THE RESOURCEFUL TEACHER

Seeds of confidence

Verónica de Andrés
Jane Arnold

Self-esteem activities for the EFL classroom

Seeds of confidence
by Verónica de Andrés and Jane Arnold

© HELBLING LANGUAGES 2009
www.helblinglanguages.com

All rights reserved; no part of this publication may be reproduced, stored in a retrieval system, or transmitted in any form or by any means, electronic, mechanical, photocopying, recording, or otherwise, without the prior written permission of the Publishers.

First published 2009
ISBN 978-3-85272-200-9

Copy edited by Caroline Petherick
Designed by Gabby Design
Cover by Capolinea
Illustrations by Roberto Battestini
Printed by Bieffe

The publishers would like to thank these sources for their kind permission to reproduce the following copyright material:
Robert Fulghum, for the poem 'All I Really Need To Know I Learned In
Kindergarten' © Robert Fulghum, p. 154.
Robert Reasoner, for material which was adapted in the brief suggestions at the beginning of each chapter and in the teachers' self-evaluation forms, pp. 179–183.
Jane Revell and Susan Norman, for the Asclepius story from 'In Your Hands: NLP in
ELT', 1997 (Saffire Press), p. 135.
SUNY Press, for the text from Neihardt's 'Black Elk Speaks', p. 69.
Science & Behavior Books, for the poem 'Be as you are' by Fritz Perls, p. 60.
Confidence Time Productions, for the poem on p. 160.
Shutterstock, for pictures on pp. 98, 119 and 163.
United Feature Syndicate ©UFS. Inc./Distribution Adnkronos, for cartoon on p. 39.
David Kettlewell, for the music for the activities on pp. 80, 82, 87, 94, 120, 138, 155 and 171 and the videos for the activities on pp. 25 and 58.
Ramón García Tamarán, for the music for the activities on pp. 24, 28, 85, 122 and 131.
Carlos Crespo (Mundoficción) and José Tomé (Sonoris) for the video for the activity on p. 28.
The sculpture in the video is by Marcelo Arce.

Every effort has been made to trace the owners of any copyright material in this book.
If notified, the publisher will be pleased to rectify any errors or omissions.

To the teachers of the world who want to make their students shine!

Our deepest fear is not that we are inadequate. Our deepest fear is that we are powerful beyond measure. It is our light, not our darkness that most frightens us. We ask ourselves, Who am I to be brilliant, gorgeous, talented, fabulous? Actually, who are you not to be?
                                                            Marianne Williamson

Our thanks go to:

The staff at Helbling for inspiring confidence at every stage in the process.
Our students and participants in seminars and workshops, from whom we got the inspiration to share these activities with others.

Thanks also to:

Bob Reasoner, for his ground-breaking work in self-esteem and education, and for making his material available to us for this book.
Jack Canfield, from whom I have learned so much, for his sustained support, and for being a major inspiration for many of these activities.
Grethe Hooper Hansen, for her example and encouragement over the years.
David Kettlewell, for creating beauty in the form of art.
And finally, my family – Héctor, Florencia, María Sol and Agustin – for being my best confidence builders.

Verónica

Earl Stevick, for the seeds of affective factors in language learning he planted.
Carmen Fonseca, Adrian Underhill and Izabella Hearn for providing insights into important aspects of teaching and living.
My children – Marcos, Carlos and Blanca – for many, many reasons.

Jane

Contents

Introduction: why is self-confidence so important in language learning? ... 8
   Coming to an understanding of self-esteem ... 9
   Answers to criticism of work with self-esteem ... 12
   Ideal selves and motivation ... 13
   Suggestions for using this book ... 14

CHAPTER 1: A SENSE OF SECURITY ... 19
   1.1 Routines ... 22
   1.2 What's your name? ... 24
   1.3 Seeds of confidence ... 26
   1.4 1, 2, 3, stare! ... 27
   1.5 A focused mind ... 28
   1.6 How do you frighten yourself? ... 30
   1.7 Listen to me ... 32
   1.8 Welcoming exams ... 34
   1.9 My mistake ... 36
   1.10 Words that open, words that close ... 38
   1.11 The rules of the game ... 40
   1.12 My coat of arms ... 41

CHAPTER 2: A SENSE OF IDENTITY ... 45
   2.1 We bingo ... 48
   2.2 Student of the week ... 51
   2.3 True and false ... 53
   2.4 Talking about me ... 54
   2.5 Circle time ... 56
   2.6 Be yourself ... 59
   2.7 A commercial about yourself ... 61
   2.8 A two-minute interview ... 63
   2.9 Magic combs ... 65
   2.10 The talking stick ... 67
   2.11 Who are you three? ... 71

CHAPTER 3: A SENSE OF BELONGING ... 75
   3.1 Mirroring ... 78
   3.2 Back to back ... 80
   3.3 Groups or pairs ... 81
   3.4 Marching together ... 82
   3.5 Line-ups ... 83
   3.6 Role-playing conflicts ... 84
   3.7 Take the weight off your shoulders ... 85
   3.8 Blindfold walk ... 86
   3.9 The confidence corridor ... 87

Contents

3.10	Hot potato	89
3.11	Statues	90
3.12	Body shop	92
3.13	The leaders dance	94
3.14	Signs of the zodiac	95
3.15	We perform	97
3.16	Today's menu	98

CHAPTER 4: A SENSE OF PURPOSE — 103

4.1	Backward buildup	105
4.2	Help yourself	107
4.3	Words of affirmation	110
4.4	Inspiring quotations	112
4.5	Eyes on the goal	115
4.6	Formula for success	117
4.7	Great dreams	120
4.8	What makes your heart sing?	122
4.9	Turning dreams into smart goals	124
4.10	Visualise your goals	127
4.11	Seeing your language self	129
4.12	A world of values	131
4.13	We can choose	133
4.14	My mission/life purpose statement	137
4.15	The end	138

CHAPTER 5: A SENSE OF COMPETENCE — 143

5.1	A/B success sharing	146
5.2	Words have power!	147
5.3	Turning points: connecting the dots	149
5.4	What I know	152
5.5	My success log	155
5.6	Appreciation works!	156
5.7	A letter of acknowledgement	158
5.8	The attitude of gratitude	160
5.9	A gift for you	162
5.10	A happy day!	164
5.11	The magic minute	166
5.12	It's your choice	168
5.13	Ping pong of talents	170
5.14	My strengths	172

Contents

APPENDIX:	Going Beyond	177
	Teacher's self-evaluation: Establishing a Sense of Security	179
	Teacher's self-evaluation: Establishing a Sense of Identity	180
	Teacher's self-evaluation: Establishing a Sense of Belonging	181
	Teacher's self-evaluation: Establishing a Sense of Purpose	182
	Teacher's self-evaluation: Establishing a Sense of Competence	183
	References and further reading	184
	Teacher's quick-reference guide	186

Introduction:
Why is self-confidence so important in language learning?

Buenos Aires, Argentina, 1993: Juan, an eight-year-old boy, was the class bully. Rejected by classmates, feared by his teachers, and constantly in trouble, he drew this picture of himself.

A programme called 'I'm Glad I'm Me' (Andrés 1999, 2007), which incorporated self-esteem activities in Juan's English as a Foreign Language class as part of a research project, was carried out over three months. At the end of that time, Juan had made surprising advances in language learning, and there was a radical change in his behaviour. His new sense of self-confidence gave him strength and he actually became very open to himself and to others. This was the way he saw himself then:

Under his second picture he wrote, 'I discovered that I am normal.'

In this picture you can see the friendly smile on his face and his arms wide open, indicating that he is no longer feeling attacked by others, as bullies often do.

Today, there can be no doubt about the importance to learning of 'affect', which refers basically to our feelings, emotions, moods and attitudes. As Rodríguez, Plax and Kearney (1996:297) say, 'Affect is, by definition, an intrinsic motivator. Positive affect sustains involvement and deepens interest in the subject matter'. Moskowitz (1999:178) points out that our students are more likely to do well when we incorporate activities which, while providing good language practice, take affect into account by supporting self-esteem or developing positive relationships. She stresses that using these types of activities 'is not to the neglect of the target language, but to the enhancement of it'.

Stevick (1980:4) emphasised the role of affect in foreign language learning, and at the same time established a useful way to conceptualise it in the classroom, when he wrote that in language learning 'success ... depends less on materials, techniques and linguistic analyses and more on what goes on inside and between the people in the classroom'. Affect, then, may relate to the relationships established in the learning context *between* students, and *between* teacher and students. It may also relate to the *inside* – to learner-internal aspects – and one of the most prominent of these aspects is self-esteem. As learners, our self-concept (our perception of ourselves, what we see when we look 'inside') and our self-esteem (our evaluation of this self-concept and our affective experience of it) are closely related to our learning. Human beings inevitably form, at all times and in all places, an image of the 'self'. How we evaluate that self – negatively or positively – will determine our self-esteem, and in the classroom this can have a highly significant influence on our learning.

Coming to an understanding of self-esteem

Self-esteem can be defined basically as confidence in our own potential. However, in a comprehensive review of the literature on self-esteem, the notion of the self often appears vague and ambiguous. To avoid misunderstandings about self-esteem when applied in the context of language learning, here is a brief journey through the history of the concept.

For centuries, the concept of the self had been left to the realms of philosophy, but in 1890 William James, in his *Principles of Psychology*, restructured that concept from the perspective of psychology. To him, the self is the result of the process of an infant developing from a state of confusion to an eventual adult state of self-awareness. He pointed out the discrepancy between the ideal self and the perceived self or self-image; the gap between them can be considered as a measure of a person's self-esteem – so the closer one's self-image is to the ideal self, the healthier one's self-esteem. Soon after this, Cooley, in his *Looking-Glass Theory of Self*, brought in the importance of reflections received from outside – feedback from others and the environment. An important implication of this is that, for young children especially, teachers act as mirrors through which they see themselves. If what the children perceive as their teacher's opinion of them is not good, they may consider themselves worthless and respond accordingly.

Humanistic psychologist Carl Rogers (1969) stressed the significance of our social needs, the most important being the need to receive a *positive regard* from others. Unfortunately, it is often the case that the need for positive regard is neglected in the classroom, and in fact is sometimes totally ignored in the search for high standards, achievement and controlled behaviour. The outcome of this neglect is the reverse of what is intended, since it often includes pointing out negative behaviour to students, not recognising the fact that *what we pay attention to we reinforce.*

Coopersmith (1967) reported that in the first grade (age 5-6), children's self-concept was a predictor of their ability to read. He defined self-esteem in terms of how we evaluate ourselves and our characteristics, the personal judgement of worthiness that is expressed in attitudes we hold toward ourselves. According to him, a child's self-image is formed by the repeated responses received from the significant others: parents first, teachers next and peers later on. As an outcome of his research, he developed a list of 'warning signals' considered to be indicators of low self-esteem, including: fearfulness and timidity, bullying and arrogance, indecision, pessimism, and reluctance to express opinions.

It was not, however, until the late 1970s that self-esteem in academic contexts became an issue of consistent study. Educators and researchers began to investigate the link between self-esteem and failure or success at school. In 1989, Dr Martin Covington at the University of California in Berkeley carried out an extensive review of the research on the relationship of self-esteem to academic achievement. He found that this research showed that higher self-esteem was consistently associated with higher achievement scores. However, among the most important conclusions for educators was the finding that it is possible to modify self-esteem through direct instruction, and that this can lead to achievement gains.

Writing specifically about language acquisition, Krashen (1985) argues that a non-threatening classroom atmosphere fosters self-confidence, and that high motivation is vital. Comprehensible input or a meaningful message is necessary, but not enough: the learner needs to be open to that input. This will not be possible if the 'affective filter' is up and the acquirer is unmotivated, lacking self-confidence, or feeling afraid of making mistakes or of being humiliated in front of others; in short, when the learner considers that the language class is a place where his or her weaknesses will be revealed.

Work done along these lines on the topic of teacher confirmation is very revealing. Researching the area of communication studies, highly relevant to the language teaching context, Ellis (2000:265) defines teacher confirmation as 'the process by which teachers communicate to students that they are valuable, significant individuals'. Applying this concept to the foreign language setting, in a study of 114 students of English in state school secondary education in Spain, León (2005) elicited a scale of teacher behaviours which made students feel confirmed – which, in other words, supported their self-esteem. The ten teacher behaviours most often mentioned were:

- congratulates students verbally and non-verbally when they do something well
- gives students confidence in their abilities, encouraging them to make an effort to improve
- pays attention to what the student does or says, listening carefully
- smiles often
- verbally transmits his or her satisfaction in students' achievements
- shows interest in answering students' questions
- is interested in students' lives, asking questions about their problems, projects and aspirations
- checks to see if students have understood explanations
- maintains eye contact with students during the class
- gives students help when they need it, being available outside class.

An interesting point in related research (Piñol 2007) is that when teachers incorporated 'confirming behaviours' into their teaching repertoire, students' attitudes changed quite dramatically. In this study, when ELT teachers consciously used confirming behaviour in class, after only a month students reported being twice as comfortable using English in class and twice as willing to express themselves freely, as well as doubling their interest in English. The implication is that when students feel accepted and their self-esteem is enhanced, their attitudes improve.

Puchta (1999:256-7) has stressed the importance of beliefs for any learning experience: 'Beliefs act as very strong filters of reality ... Our learners' beliefs are often related to past experiences, but they also form blueprints for future behaviour'. It is because beliefs operate at the level of our identity that they are so very influential in the learning process. Thus, for example, if we correct students' errors in an insensitive manner, what they may perceive is not that we have given them an opportunity to see how to improve their competence in the target language, but instead that we have reinforced their belief that they are not capable of learning the language or even that they are not valuable human beings. So their identity and their self-esteem are compromised, they may become unwilling to try again, and their future learning experiences are less likely to be productive.

Students who have formed a belief that they can't learn languages are right. They can't! – unless they change this belief. Puchta

(1999:257) maintains that 'negative beliefs influence our students' expectations. Low expectations lead to a low level of motivation and every failure is seen as confirmation of the initial beliefs'. Their inner speech or self-talk may go something like this: 'I'm right again; I'm a terrible language learner – I knew it right from the start.' The feeling that is generated does not depend on objective, observable facts but on our beliefs, often very subjective – but fortunately, for this very reason, they are also amenable to change.

Answers to criticism of work with self-esteem

The incorporation of concern with self-esteem has proved to be an important direction in education. Yet in the process it may at times have come to be considered a band-wagon to jump on or even a panacea which is alleged to have the ability to solve complex problems that have very diverse and unrelated roots. Thus, there have been misunderstandings of the essence of the work on self-esteem in education. Critics have affirmed that dealing with self-esteem can lead to egocentric behaviour and to unrealistic expectations; however, for productive work in the classroom it is essential to realise that what is being considered is what we could term 'healthy' self-esteem, where students have both a **positive and accurate belief** about themselves and their abilities, and also the **commitment and responsibility** that comes when they see themselves as able to complete worthwhile goals.

Robert Reasoner, founder and former president of the International Council for Self-Esteem, explains clearly that self-esteem programmes are not about simply making students feel good. He stresses that efforts like that are not likely to have lasting effects, 'because they fail to strengthen the internal sources of self-esteem related to integrity, responsibility and achievement. Only by addressing these areas can one effectively build self-esteem' (Reasoner, 1992:24).

So it is **never** a case of giving students false beliefs or of telling them that 'anything goes'. Nor is it, as some have affirmed, a case of creating an unhealthy ego. What we are referring to is a balanced view of self-worth from which it is easier to carry out learning tasks. The reason for being concerned in the classroom with self-esteem and other affective issues is to provide a supportive atmosphere in which we can better encourage learners to work hard to reach their learning potential, unhindered by the negative affect Krashen referred to with his metaphor of the 'affective filter'.

Concern with affective factors in the classroom is strongly supported by implications from neurobiology as well as by language policy makers. The Council of Europe's *Common European Framework of Reference* emphasises that one of the necessary areas to deal with in language teaching is 'existential competence' (*savoir-être*), which includes attitudes, motivation, values, self-confidence and self-esteem; these are considered to be strong influences on learner roles in communicative acts and even on their ability to learn.

Ideal selves and motivation

Related to the absence of motivation, a weak self-concept makes it hard to be fully on task, as energy is split between the task and an excessive concern about one's lack of ability or worth. This creates a doubly disadvantaged language-learning situation: first, there is less energy for the task in hand, and second, the negative feelings generated make the learning experience unpleasant and less motivating, and thus less effective. Ehrman and Dörnyei (1998:257) point out that according to current theories on motivation, 'the highest human priority is the need for self-acceptance'. Thus, we cannot ignore this factor in any activity that is as motivation-dependent as language learning.

In language learning, motivation is a key issue, and the walls of staff rooms are mute witnesses to frequent teacher complaints about lack of student motivation. Yet, through work related to the self, there are interesting options for developing greater motivation. As Markus and Ruvolo (1989:213) claim, 'imagining one's own actions through the construction of elaborated possible selves achieving the desired goal may ... directly facilitate the translation of goals into intentions and instrumental actions'.

Applying this idea to language learning, Dörnyei (2005:106) concludes that 'if the person we would like to become speaks an L2, the *ideal L2 self* is a powerful motivator to learn the L2 because of the desire to reduce the discrepancy between our actual and ideal selves'. Thus, if in our students' image of the self they want to become they include an aspect of successful language learning, this can provide strong support for the learning process.

Teachers can help to develop this self-image by on the one hand helping to make being an L2 speaker seem **attractive**, and on the other hand making it seem **possible**. They can do this through encouragement, and by stressing that if learners are willing to work to learn the L2, they will be successful in doing so. (See Murphey 2006 for suggestions for helping them learn more effectively.)

Some very good news is that there is no doubt that self-esteem can be nurtured through successful learning experiences, which enable learners to see themselves as competent; students that feel this way are likely to be more highly motivated and to take the risks and meet the challenges involved in the learning process, and enjoy the outcomes. This is coherent with Nathaniel Branden's (1994:27) widely accepted definition of self-esteem: 'the disposition to experience oneself as competent to cope with life's challenges and being worthy of happiness'.

Self-esteem activities can be a vehicle for improving language acquisition, and at the same time can help to fulfil broader educational goals. Today's students live in an extremely complex and changing world. Even very young children have to learn how to cope with academic challenges as well as many other issues on a personal and social level. So in times of rising social conflicts, many of which are directly concerned with youth, instead of asking ourselves if we should work with self-esteem in the classroom, we might consider what Reasoner (1992:30) says: 'The question should be, do we have a choice? Self-esteem cannot be considered the panacea to all problems in the classroom, yet it may well be our hope for a better world.'

Suggestions for using this book

Seeds of Confidence has been organised around the model of self-esteem developed by Robert Reasoner (1982). The five components in his model are Security, Identity, Belonging, Purpose and Competence. One chapter of the book is dedicated to each of these components, with a presentation of the component and activities for developing it in the language classroom.

Each chapter starts with a list of short suggestions for dealing with the component in the classroom. While some of these ideas focus mainly on establishing a productive learning atmosphere, others can be adapted for language practice as well.

Suggestions for levels are given, but do not feel restricted by these. Many are actually one-size-fits-all activities and can be adapted for use with levels lower than those specified, especially if you use the L1 for parts of the exercise. You are the best judge of which activities would work in your class, and if an entire activity is too easy or too difficult there may be some aspects of it which you would like to keep and modify to fit your context.

The importance of developing a respectful classroom atmosphere is dealt with in different parts of the book, and suggestions are made for doing so. While many activities in the book can be used productively as 'ice-breakers' to help students get to know each other, we also point out that other activities may work best when the group is already 'warmed up', when students feel more comfortable together. Again, the learning context always needs to be taken into consideration.

Many of these activities can be used in other subject-matter classes, either to establish a productive group atmosphere or to support CLIL/bilingual teaching. You are encouraged to share activities with your colleagues in other teaching areas; for example, **Turning points: connecting the dots** (Activity 5.3) could be adapted to work with learning about someone who has made a significant contribution in any area of the curriculum.

Several activities using visualisation have been included. Mental imagery is very useful for many aspects of the language-learning process (see Arnold, Puchta and Rinvolucri 2007) and can connect with Dörnyei's 'Ideal Self' model of motivation. However, if your students haven't worked with visualisation or imagery before, you might want to introduce these activities gradually. Guide the visualisation in a slow, quiet voice which helps students to relax and 'go inside'. We can access our inner imagery more easily if we close our eyes, and you can suggest that your students do this – but if some are uncomfortable doing so, ask them just to look down.

You are encouraged to work with the activities in the book as a reflective practitioner. To facilitate this, in the Appendix there is a self-evaluation form for each component dealt with, and in the bibliography you will find some suggestions for further reading.

Finally, we suggest that these activities be used in a consistent manner. They are designed to be used not merely as fillers on a Friday afternoon, but as an integral part of the language class. Benefits, both for students' self-esteem and for language learning, are accumulative. If we as teachers become fully aware of the importance to the learning process of student's self-concept, then ways to enhance it that we are comfortable with in our classes will present themselves – and, as an added benefit, our own self-concept will be strengthened in the process.

A CD-ROM containing music, worksheets and other material is included.

CHAPTER 1
A SENSE OF SECURITY

There are only two lasting bequests we can hope to give our children. One is roots; the other, wings.

Hodding Carter

Chapter 1: A Sense of Security

A sense of security – both physical and emotional – is a basic human need that implies knowing what is expected from us, feeling safe and capable of trusting others, and knowing that others can trust us. It also involves understanding and accepting the need for rules and limits.

For security, the idea of limits is very important. Limits need to be established by mutual agreement, and it is understood that they are there to give us security. When we are driving down a highway, if there are no signs, no markings, the trip could be more difficult and dangerous; the same is true in the classroom. We need, however, to differentiate between rules as limits and rules as punishment. Often the latter are reactive and imposed, and enforced in a way that makes students feel bad, feel guilty; whereas rules as limits are proactive and agreed upon, and are there to protect us and make us aware of the most effective ways of behaving.

In language learning an important consideration is that in order to learn to speak a language we inevitably make mistakes, and so in a language class establishing the sense of security is especially necessary. Here we could learn from Steve Jobs, founder of Apple. When asked how Apple was so successful, his answer was that they hire great people and create the type of environment where people can grow and make mistakes (Borba, 1993).

> **The Sense of Security**
> leads to confidence based on physical and emotional security.
> It provides the necessary support for developing self-knowledge.
>
> **Teachers who promote a sense of security:**
> - define procedures and routines (so learners know what is expected of them).
> - involve learners in defining rules and norms.
> - enforce rules in ways that supports learners' self-respect.
> - promote individual responsibility.

Suggestions for Building a Sense of Security

☐ Involve students in setting classroom rules that create a safe and positive learning climate for everyone.

☐ Establish a procedure for students to meet with you privately when they have something they want to discuss with you. You might set aside some time each week when students can sign up for an uninterrupted conference of around 3–5 minutes with you. This time can be used for students to share their concerns or ask for help with a specific problem.

☐ Talk with students – individually or as a class – about their concerns at school, and brainstorm ways they might deal with them.

- Develop classroom traditions (for celebrating birthdays, recognising exceptional work, greeting and integrating new students etc.); the familiar brings a sense of security.

- Use disciplinary procedures that, rather than merely administering punishments, help students make better decisions. Use the natural law of cause and effect, where if one misbehaves there will be established consequences.

- Develop individual contracts for those students who have difficulty conforming to classroom behaviour standards. Include in the contract the standards of expected behaviour, student commitments to agreed standards and the consequences (see above) of failing to meet standards.

- Make it safe for students to risk asking a question or giving an answer without being ridiculed or laughed at.

- Be clear with students about your expectations and standards and why those are important to you.

- Take time at the beginning of the year to make certain that students know each other's names (See **What's your name?**, Activity 1.2) and get to know something about each other.

- Avoid forms of punishment or lecturing that might in any way intimidate a student.

- When useful and possible, hold class meetings to address issues that may be worrying the students.

- Establish procedures so that students always know where they can find out about homework or class assignments.

- Find ways to show a sense of trust in your students.

- Display a list of desirable behaviours for students (see **The rules of the game**, Activity 1.11)

- Establish routines for such things as entering and leaving the classroom, handing in and passing out papers, collecting and distributing materials, and correcting exercises, so that procedures are well understood.

- Help students to identify their fears. Then create different possible scenarios or role-playing activities with the class, in order to help students realise that outcomes other than the ones they fear are possible.

- Develop a secret signal, such as a thumbs-up or a peace sign (or whatever would be a positive sign in the culture you are in), that can be used with students to remind them of their commitment to meet classroom standards. Explain that the secret signal conveys your confidence in their ability to comply with those standards.

- Recognise students who by improving their behaviour contribute to a more positive classroom atmosphere. As a reward you might, if appropriate, let them take home an interesting book, magazine or DVD in English, or let them use a special computer program.

- Help them to learn to work with timetables or other visual ways to use their time more productively.

- Periodically review classroom standards with the class, and make any necessary revisions to them, rather than assume that all students know them.

- If new students come to your classroom, encourage other students to go over the classroom rules with them and explain the justification for having the rules.

- When working with students who are frequently in trouble, be sure to recognise whenever you can the student's traits or accomplishments for which they have reason to be proud.

- Catch students doing something good: changing behaviour is much easier using a positive rather than a negative approach. (Ask them to write a Good News Report, give them a Positive Performers Award ...)

- Use **Think-Pair-Share (T-P-S)** from the cooperative learning approach (Kagan 1994). This teaching technique helps students feel much more secure when speaking in front of others. If we just throw out questions for students to answer point blank in front of the class, it generally produces anxiety and a weak response – whereas the T-P-S technique gives students a sense of security, because they have time to think before speaking.
How does it work? Present to your students a question you want them to answer, or a topic for discussion; have them **think** on their own first, then in **pairs** exchange ideas; and only after they have had time to get their ideas together and practise a bit do you ask them to **share** with the whole class.
This technique can be used often, and will facilitate the production of more sophisticated ideas and better language use.

> **Students can learn better in a caring environment where they are treated with respect, where limits are clearly defined, where they know what is expected from them, and where the rules defining rights and responsibilities are consistently enforced in positive ways.**

1.1 Routines

Focus: Routines convey a sense of security, of knowing what to expect. These brief activities can help to build this sense of security and to begin the class on a positive note, thus opening the way to learning.

Level: Lower intermediate +

Time: 10 minutes for each of A, B and C

Preparation: None.

in class

A Something Good and New

1. Students sit or stand in a circle. Invite them to share something that is new and good for them; it can be related to their learning or their family and friends or something they did or read in the last week that had a positive impact on them.
   The best way to do this is for you to go first; stand in the circle and begin with something new and good for you. For example, 'Something new and good is that I have a friend coming to visit me this weekend' (or 'I went out to dinner for my birthday yesterday', or 'I had a good talk with another teacher'…), and then pass a little ball to the student on your left for him or her to continue sharing.

2. This can be repeated any time you think your students would enjoy doing it again.

B The News of the Day

1. Welcome your students with a smile as they come in through the doors. This will give them a feeling of warmth and appreciation: your students will feel connected from the very first moment they see you!

2. Invite them to sit in a circle, and put up a sign that says *The News of the Day*. During this activity, they are invited to share something going on in their life at that moment. Begin by modelling your news, saying 'My news of the day is that …'. What you say can be about something important that is going to happen or that has happened to you, or just something ordinary that you plan to do. Then the student sitting next to you speaks, or you can toss a little ball round the class to select speakers at random. Especially at the beginning of the term, you may want to encourage students to share positive news. This routine is very good for helping students to open up to the rest of the class by sharing something about their lives.

1.1 Routines

C Question of the Day

1. This can be used as a daily routine for you to learn more about your students and also to let them get to know more about each other, so they will feel more comfortable in class. You can ask them a question about a favourite food, sport, hobby, wish, or other question relevant to their age and interests, such as:
   - ☐ What do you like to do after school?
   - ☐ Where do you play?
   - ☐ Do you have pets?
   - ☐ What do you do when you are happy?
   - ☐ What do you do when you feel sad?
   - ☐ What do you like to do at weekends?

2. After asking the question, go around the circle or throw a little ball to get answers from several students. If you have time, and if the students are participating actively, consider asking another question or two.

Variations

1. Students can take turns to choose the questions themselves, and then ask them to the rest of the class. They can be encouraged to ask more sophisticated autobiographical questions such as:
   - ☐ What do you see yourself doing in 10 years' time?
   - ☐ What is your major goal?
   - ☐ What does friendship mean to you?
   - ☐ What do you like most about your class?
   - ☐ Who is your hero in life?

2. We have also found the following to be very successful: at the beginning of the course, give students a strip of paper each and have them write on it an interesting question they would like to be asked or wouldn't mind being asked. Pick up the strips, select one of the questions and ask it to everyone in the class, and save the rest to begin class with periodically during the rest of the term. Some questions our students have contributed: *What do you like to do when nobody is looking at you? Where would you like to be right now? What makes you feel happy? What aspect of your personality would you like to change? What kind of person are you? What is your favourite place in the world?*

1.2 What's your name?

Focus: Learning students' names

Level: Elementary +, depending on the suggestion

Time: 5–10 minutes

Preparation: For the second activity, bring a CD player to play Track 1 of the CD or some background music your students will like; a supply of labels or post-it notes.

At the beginning of the school year, it is well worth spending a few minutes during the early classes to do activities which can help you to learn students' names, and help them get to know each other. Here are some suggestions for some common ways to do this; you may want to use more than one on different days.

in class

➢ For real beginners, you can pre-teach them the basic language for asking someone's name and answering, and then have them stand in a circle to take turns asking the question and throwing a small ball to someone else for them to answer. Tell them that once they have asked and answered, they step back out of the circle. This way, everyone gets the chance to say their name.

➢ The first day of class, give each student a label or a post-it, and ask them to write their name and draw a quick picture of something related to them in some way, or something they like, etc. Then they stick these onto themselves, and with the music playing, they walk around looking at each other's names and at the pictures their classmates have drawn. At a signal (you can stop the music or clap) they then will stop and pair with another student, and try to guess what the picture means or says about the person. They could say 'I think you like travelling' or 'You enjoy meeting people', and the student who did the drawing can tell them if they are right – and if not, they can tell them what the drawing means for them. Give them time to talk to several others – and you participate too.

➢ Have students standing in two parallel lines. They should think of something related to them that starts with the same letter as their first name. It doesn't really have to be true, and silly examples are good; the idea is to have a memory peg to hook the name onto. Then start at the beginning of one line, and the first person says, 'My name is Pierre and I like potatoes (am patient, practise, play tennis ...)' then the next person says, 'He is Pierre and he likes potatoes, and my name is Ina and I write with ink (eat ice-cream, like to ice skate, am interesting'). Go down the first line with each person repeating what the person immediately before them in the

1.2 What's your name?

line has said, and then adding their contribution. Then the other line starts the same way with the names in their line. When they have finished, tell them in a light-hearted way that you are going to give them a special test, but you will let them have a few minutes to study for it. Explain that each line will have to know the names of everyone in the other line, but the students can talk a moment with the people next to them to see if together they can remember the names. Then ask for volunteers in one line, and then the other, to try to name everyone in the other line. Clap when each volunteer finishes. This quick activity helps your students – AND YOU! – to learn the names of everyone in the class.

➢ Pair students randomly and give them 5 minutes to find out something interesting about the other person. Then, in a circle, each person tells one thing about their partner, saying their partner's name first ('Carla has a collection of stamps from all the countries in Europe, and she wants to visit each country some day,') and ending with 'That is something I learned about Carla.' That way, you will hear each person's name twice. An added benefit is that you and the students learn something about that student.

➢ At the beginning of the year, before your students really know each other, when you put them in groups of four or five to do an activity, tell them that they need to be sure to learn each other's names first because you are going to walk around while they are working and check to see if they know the name of everyone in their group. You can jokingly warn them that something awful will happen to them if they don't know all the names. Let them work for a while, and then go to one group and have a student give all their names. If you think you won't remember the names, have a second student repeat the names. Then as you walk around, mentally rehearse the names in this group so you know them well before you go to another group and do the same. You can perhaps try to make associations in your mind to help you remember the names. Some teachers have learned the names of all the students in a large class this way in only 10 minutes!

➢ Put digital photos of all the students onto a page of an interactive whiteboard and write their names scrambled on the board. Call on different students to come to the board and try to drag names of three of their classmates to match their photos.

Note
When we use our students' names, we are sending them a very important message: I recognise you as a worthwhile human being; I don't consider you just a number on my attendance list. (On the other hand, if students are misbehaving it is much easier to redirect their behaviour if we can use their names to get their attention!)

1.3 Seeds of confidence

Focus: Gap filling; writing. This activity helps learners become more centred.

Level: Intermediate +

Time: 30-40 minutes

Preparation: Have the presentation on the CD ready to project from your computer.
One copy of worksheet for each student.

in class

1. Hand out the worksheets and ask the students to fill in the gaps individually in a way they feel would be appropriate, and then compare with a classmate.

2. Tell the students to turn over their worksheets and just watch and listen, then play the presentation once. After this, have them look at their worksheets and from memory try to see if what they had written was correct. Play it a second time, having them check their worksheets.

3. Optional: working in groups of 3 to 5, they choose one of the three quotations and write a short dialogue or little story in which the chosen quotation is the moral of the story. Tell them not to mention the one they have picked. Then each group reads theirs, and the class guesses what would be the quotation/moral of the story.

We know what we are but we know not

_____

(William Shakespeare)

Believe in yourself! Have faith in your

_____

(Norman Vincent Peale)

When _____ and _____ work together, expect a masterpiece.

(John Ruskin)

1, 2, 3, stare!

Focus: Speaking. Having fun can help to reduce fear of speaking and encourage greater participation

Level: Elementary +

Time: 5-10 minutes

Preparation: A set of cards with tasks, varied according to the age and language level of the group; see examples below.

in class

1. Ask the class to stand in a circle. Tell them that when you say '1,2,3, STARE!', everyone should stare at someone else. When two students stare at each other, the pair steps into the middle of the circle, where they will have to perform a task. (If there are several pairs, they can take turns.)

2. The pair in the middle draw two of your task cards and between them choose one of the tasks, and perform it.

3. Repeat several times.

Ask each other what is one of your favourite words in English.	Sing a song you both know in English	Ask each other about what you did yesterday
One of you names 5 parts of the body, and the other points to the part named	Talk about your favourite food	Talk about the unit/lesson you are studying
Say 5 words beginning with A	Ask each other about what you plan to do in summer	Spell each other's name in English
Each of you says something you can do well	Ask each other about someone you admire	Each of you tells about your favourite toy as a child
Discuss whether it is better to live in the city or in the country	Talk about learning English	One of you gives orders (Go to the door ...) and the other does this
Create a dialogue between assistant and customer (e.g. at the travel agent)	Discuss what makes a good friend	Discuss the advantages of holidays by the sea or in the mountains

Note
Games in a language classroom focused on self-esteem are non-competitive, so don't give points; winning is overcoming the fear of speaking and enjoying participating as part of the learning process.

1.5 A focused mind

Focus: To create a relaxed atmosphere before starting the class; to help students calm down and become grounded and focused

Level: Elementary +

Time: 5 minutes; 30 minutes with the variation

Preparation: Be prepared to project the video presentation of the words below. Alternatively, bring in a CD player and some relaxing background music.

in class

1. Tell your students that you are going to do an exercise that will help them to be calm and focused, and to relax. Ask them to let go, for a moment, of things they might be thinking about, and simply focus their attention on their breathing.

2. After a few moments, either project the CD video from the computer or say the following words and play your music. For elementary level you can pre-teach any of the words they don't know:
   In-Out (pause)
   Deep-Slow (pause)
   Calm-Ease (pause)
   Smile-Release (pause)

   You can repeat these words three or four times, whatever seems right for your class. And remember: a still mind is a focused mind; a focused mind is an alert mind; and an alert mind is what we need for learning!

Variation
When you have done this a few times with your class, you can give out the chart below, or put it on the board and ask them to work in groups of 4 to think of other words they might like to use to help them feel good and relax when they begin class. This can be done as a cooperative learning task (Kagan 1994) with:
- one person as the coordinator, who gets them all participating;
- another the scribe, who writes down the suggestions and then the final version;
- another, the language monitor, who both makes sure everyone speaks in the target language while working and then – consulting you if necessary – checks to be sure the language is correctly written;
- and finally the presenter. Every day you can have the presenter from one of the groups do the focusing exercise with the class.

You can also suggest to your students that they individually choose the set of words they like best, and learn it, to use when they are feeling nervous or stressed at any time

1.5 A focused mind

		(pause)
		(pause)
		(pause)
		(pause)

Acknowledgement
The words used in Step 2 above are from **Thich Nhat Hanh**, the Vietnamese Zen Master and poet who was proposed by Martin Luther King for the Nobel Peace Prize.

1.6 How do you frighten yourself?

Focus: Speaking and writing. To give students a sense of security by enabling them to discuss their fears. This activity aims to create an outlet for your students to express their fears, as one way of letting go of them, and also to promote a sense of respect for each other. This activity is best done when a supportive atmosphere has been established.

Level: Intermediate +

Time: 50 minutes

Preparation: Decide how many groups to divide your class into; bring in enough small objects, such as sea shells or interesting stones, for each group to have one.
Provide A3 paper, coloured pens, etc.

in class

1. Write on the board:

   # F E A R

   Tell your students to try to guess something that each letter could stand for.

2. Allow a few minutes of brainstorming, and then tell them that one possible interpretation could be the following: F stands for Fantasised, E for Experiences, A for Appearing, and the R for Real. Continue by explaining that most of our fears are things we imagine, that have not taken place ... so they are Fantasised Experiences Appearing Real. Explain briefly that when we scare ourselves this way, we are likely to make our fears become real. (For lower levels this can be explained in the L1.)

3. Ask students to think of a few ways they would be willing to share that they could complete the following statement:

   > I frighten myself by imagining that ...

   In order to encourage them to open up, it is important that you model the activity, giving a few examples of your own, e.g.
   One way I frighten myself is by imagining that if I ask for what I want, people will be upset with me, or say no.
   One way I frighten myself is by imagining that something bad can happen to my children.
   One way I frighten myself is by imagining that I will have problems that I can't solve.

1.6 How do you frighten yourself?

4. Have students get into groups of 5 or 6: give each group an object, then explain the following procedure:
   - Only the person holding the special object can speak. The first person will say one of their examples to the others in the group.
   - When that person has finished speaking, he or she passes the object to the student on his/her left
   - Continue until all the people in each circle have had a chance to talk, and then go around once or twice more.

   Some important considerations:
   - **I pass**: tell your students that they can say 'I pass' if they wish, so there is no obligation to speak. Far from discouraging them to participate, this creates a feeling of respect and intimacy, and usually by the time they get to the third round, most of the students will have participated.
   - **All that is said here is confidential**: agree with your students about the need to keep confidentiality about anything spoken during this activity.
   - **No put-downs**: tell your students that this means everyone listens with heart and head, with respect. You can also say **Poker face**, which means that your students should remain as neutral as possible while they are listening to what is said in the circle – no indications of disagreement or agreement.

5. Tell your students to appoint a secretary to jot down the most important things said, and then with this material each group can make a mind map (see Activity 2.5), or write a paragraph, or prepare a drawing, using the paper and pens you have supplied, to be presented to the rest of the class.
   This part of the activity is important, as it will allow everyone to notice that our FEARS are more common than we imagine. You can even encourage your students to analyze their answers in order to cluster them in some way.

6. Finish by asking them to share any insights they may have after going through this process.

Variation for lower-level students
After they have spoken in their groups (Step 4), ask them each to write down things they said on a small piece of paper and give it to you so you can prepare a poster with a mind map entitled OUR FEARS for the following class. Include a fear of your own, and the most common ones mentioned by students.
To begin class that day, display the poster, and in pairs they can discuss which ones they both share.

1.7 Listen to me

Focus: To practise active listening

Level: Intermediate +

Time: 10-15 minutes the first time; 5 minutes if repeated

Preparation: Optional: prepare to project the Active Listening Chart.

in class

1. Have students each think of an issue, something that is bothering them or worrying them. It can also be something they are very interested in at the moment. Say it should be something they would feel comfortable talking about to another person.

2. Explain to them that listening actively to others is a very important life skill, as well as a language skill, and that this is something that doctors, business people and many others learn to do. When someone really listens to us, we feel much more willing to speak, which is obviously a very important factor in a language classroom.
   Explain the basics in the table below, projecting it from your computer if you wish. You can use your learners' L1 if necessary.

ACTIVE LISTENING
How to do it: ☐ Listen carefully to what the speaker is saying, paying attention to both their verbal and the non-verbal language (especially body language and tone of voice). ☐ Empathise – try to put yourself in their shoes – don't judge. ☐ Show interest and understanding. ☐ Stay with the speaker – listen without interrupting, communicate to them that you are really listening to what they are saying (e.g. make eye contact … lean forward a little …).

3. Students are now going to get in pairs. Have them decide who will be A and who will be B.

4. Tell them that As will begin, and they will have one minute to talk about their issue. During this time Bs are going to practise active listening. Stress that here B has the really important role. After one minute, stop them, and now Bs will speak and As will be the active listeners.

5. After this, have them discuss with their partner how it felt to speak when someone was really listening. This can also lead to a full-class discussion.

1.7 Listen to me

Follow-up
This is an activity that can be repeated several times. You can assign a topic for each student to think about for a moment, and then repeat the above procedure.

1.8 Welcoming exams

Focus: To give students a greater feeling of security when taking exams. With less anxiety, they will be able to perform better and give a closer approximation to what they actually know.

Level: Intermediate +

Time: 40-50 minutes

Preparation: For the fourth activity, make copies of the chart, or write it on the board for students to copy.

in class

Before you give your students an exam, especially an important one, spend time helping them to prepare. Try the following steps during a single class, or spaced over several days:

➢ Have a class discussion about exams. Then ask your students to think about the topic: *How I feel during an exam, and why I feel that way.* Then they make a few notes, and compare ideas with a classmate. Often, merely knowing that others feel the same as you do can help reduce anxiety.

➢ In groups of 3 to 5, students brainstorm some strategies for preparing for and doing well in exams. These can be strategies they have actually used or only just thought about.

➢ Whole class: each group reports the strategies they have listed. Make notes of these on the board. Discuss the advantages of each, and make any other suggestions you would have.

➢ Have students work individually to fill in the chart **My Next Exam**. You can write the main areas to be covered on the board first, and you may want to discuss possible test-taking strategies. When they finish, they can share what they have written with the person sitting next to them.

➢ Reform the groups: explain what categories of questions (multiple choice, true/false, short answers, translations, fill in the gaps ...) you want to use in the next exam. Tell them that they are going to write some test questions for each category, and that in the exam you will use five (or four, or three ...) of the total number of questions they have written.

➢ Give them time to work in their groups, writing the number of questions you specify. Collect these to use when you prepare the exam. You may need to make slight modifications, but try to leave them as close as possible to the students' original questions and to choose something from each one of the groups.

1.8 Welcoming exams

MY NEXT EXAM
Main areas to be covered in the exam
Areas I feel most confident about
Areas I feel I need to work most on
Strategies I am going to use to prepare for the exam

1.9 My mistake

Focus: Writing and listening.

Level: Intermediate +

Time: 40–50 minutes

Preparation: Make posters with the mistake quotations, printing one each on an A4 sheet of paper, of different colours if possible. Put them up around the classroom.

in class

1. At the beginning of the lesson, have students walk around the room to read the quotations and decide which one they like best.

2. In groups of 4 or 5, they share which quotations they chose and why. Encourage them to discuss anything of interest related to the quotations.

3. Tell the class a mistake story of yours (see example below).

4. Give students about 10 minutes to work individually and think of a time when they made a mistake and to write a short paragraph explaining what happened. Stress that they should feel comfortable telling others about it.

5. Reform groups: the group members tell each other their mistake stories. The group chooses the one they like best, and then they read it to the whole class.

6. Discuss with students the need to make mistakes in order to learn. While our goal is to speak the language we are learning fluently, for us to reach our goal we will have to use the language before we know it well, and it is normal to make mistakes.

Variation
For Step 5, collect the students' stories, and read each one out to the class. If you wish, you can make minor corrections as you read. Have the class try to guess who might have written the mistake story. After a moment, whether they guess correctly or not, say 'This is Gunter's (Alicia's ...) beautiful (or lovely, or ...) mistake.' Do this for each one, to reinforce the idea that it is all right to make mistakes.

Jane's mistake:
One day she went to class, and when she got there she noticed she had put on one black shoe and one brown one. But that isn't all. One shoe had a higher heel than the other one!

1.9 My mistake

Mistakes are the portals of discovery. (James Joyce)	The only people, scientific or other, who never make mistakes are those who do nothing. (Thomas Henry Huxley)
Freedom is not worth having if it does not include the freedom to make mistakes. (Mahatma Gandhi)	The only real mistake is the one from which we learn nothing. (John Powell.)
If I had my life to live over … I'd dare to make more mistakes next time. (Nadine Stair)	A life spent making mistakes is not only more honorable but more useful than a life spent doing nothing. (George Bernard Shaw)
Mistakes, obviously, show us what needs improving. Without mistakes, how would we know what we had to work on? (Peter McWilliams)	The greatest mistake you can make in life is to be continually fearing you will make one. (Elbert Hubbard)
Mistakes are a part of being human. Appreciate your mistakes for what they are: precious life lessons that can only be learned the hard way. (Al Franken)	A mistake is a gift to the class. (Caleb Gattegno)

Note
For students to have a useful, positive attitude towards their errors, we need to have sensitive policies of error correction.

Acknowledgement
We learned about telling mistake stories from Tim Murphey's *Language Hungry! An Introduction to Language Learning, Fun and Self-Esteem*, 2006 (Helbling Languages).

1.10 Words that open, words that close

Focus: When we say negative things to ourselves, as well as when we use pessimistic expressions, we put ourselves down. To counteract that, this activity is aimed at encouraging students to use words that open the mind by raising their awareness of the impact of certain words or expressions.

> *The mind is like a parachute; it only works when it is open.*
> (Anthony D'Angelo)

Level: Lower intermediate +

Time: 40–50 minutes

Preparation: None.

in class

1. Ask students to give you words that describe how you feel in your body when someone says negative, critical things to you. You could do this in students' L1 and then translate into English. Do the same for when someone praises you.

2. Explain to your class that this shows the power of words over our body energy. You can explain that just as negative thinking will take away your energy, so words and expressions that denote obligation, burden, and difficulty also have a negative impact on our energy level. Write these words on the board: *but, I have to, I should, I can't*. Point out how even though on the surface they don't appear critical, they affect us in a negative manner, closing our minds. This happens both when someone else says words or expressions like these to us and when we say them to ourselves. Add any similar words that your students or you can think of.

3. Then ask your students how they can replace these words with others that open the mind. Do this as a brainstorming activity. Have a volunteer write down all the words that are said. Some examples would be
   And instead of *But*
   I want to instead of *I have to*
   I choose to instead to *I should*
   I can if I work instead of *I can't*

4. As a follow-up, you can ask your students to get into groups and write a sketch, role play, story or song, using the positive and the negative words. And then have them perform them for the class.

1.10 Words that open, words that close

Note
In an old Peanuts cartoon, Charlie Brown shows how thoughts, feelings and the body are all interconnected.

1.11 The rules of the game

Focus: To create an atmosphere of trust and respect, where rules are clear and also designed in ways that will promote cooperation between students and teacher.
To teach students the importance of focusing on what we want, rather than what we don't want. This activity works best when used at the beginning of the academic year or the course.

Level: Elementary +

Time: 30-40 minutes

Preparation: None.

in class

1. Have students get into groups of 4 to 6, and think of three rules they consider important to respect in class. Allow approximately 10 minutes of discussion in the groups, and have each group appoint a secretary, who will write down the rules, to share them with the rest of the class. For lower levels, they can write the rules in their L1, and you can help them to translate the rules into English.

2. The secretaries read the rules for their groups.

3. It is very likely that many rules will be written using the negative – e.g. *Don't interrupt, Don't be late, Don't insult others* – because this is the way rules are generally presented. This will give you an opportunity to show them the importance of focusing on 'what we **want**' instead of 'what we **don't** want'. Invite them to re-write any of their rules written with *Don't* in a positive way, stressing the desired behaviour. For example, if they have written *Don't be late*, the alternative could be *Arrive on time*. Allow a few minutes for discussion, discovery and reframing, and then ask one representative of each group to report their final version of the rules to the rest of the class. As they give the rules, write them on the board or have a student do so.

4. When all rules have been presented, the students vote for the ones they consider most important for a list of class rules. A total of seven to ten rules works best. And you can always add a few that perhaps were not mentioned, if you feel it important. Have students copy the rules.

Extension
Each group can prepare a poster listing and illustrating the rules in some way. If you have, for example, six groups and six posters, for the next six days put up a new poster on the wall each day so students can internalise the rules that they have chosen as being important. If you can leave one of the posters on the wall, then any time there is an infraction of the rules, all you may need to do is point to the poster!

1.12 My coat of arms

Focus: Developing a sense of emotional security through positive feedback from others. Lexical area of personal qualities.

Level: Elementary +

Time: Lesson 1, 15 minutes; Lesson 2, 15 minutes

Preparation: Think of two adjectives, truthful and positive, to describe each student in your class, and make a list of these.
Make one enlarged photocopy of the coat of arms shield per student.
For Lesson 2, optional: bring in a music player and tape/CD of some heroic-sounding music.

in class

Lesson 1

1. Put students into groups of 3, and give each student a copy of the coat of arms. They write their name on their own paper, and in one of the four areas they write two or three positive adjectives or qualities that they feel apply to themselves. Then they pass their paper to the others in their group who each write one or two more in the second area. Lower-level students can use dictionaries to find the words they need, or ask you.

2. As each group finishes, pick up their papers, and in the third area write your two positive adjectives for each student. You might like to write them in quickly while other students are finishing or working on other classwork; or alternatively you can take the papers home to do this.

3. For the last area, students take their coat of arms home and ask a family member or friend to give them two more adjectives. They may need to translate if the person asked doesn't know English. Ask them to colour and decorate their coat of arms any way they would like, perhaps adding drawings of symbols of their qualities. Then they should bring the coat of arms in, for Lesson 2.

Lesson 2

4. Post the coats of arms around the class as if it were a museum, and let the students walk around the class, trying to find someone who shares at least two qualities with them. If you like, play the music while they are looking at their classmates' work.

1.12 My coat of arms

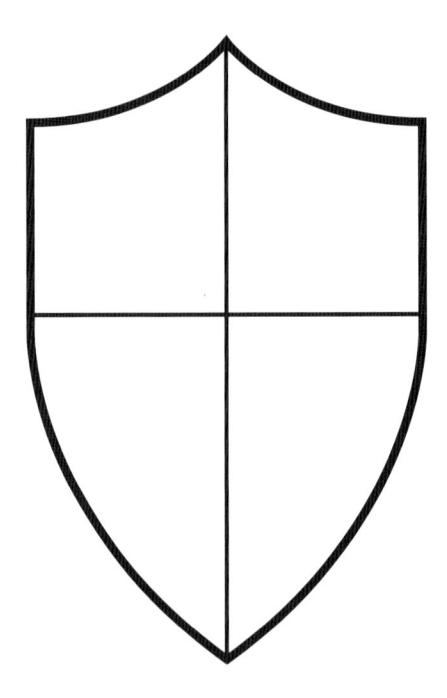

Notes
1. The coat of arms is in the shape of a shield. Shields provide security and protect us, and the positive image we have of ourselves protects us emotionally.

2. This activity is best done once the students know each other well enough to be able to supply appropriate qualities about each other.

Acknowledgement
This is a version of activity we saw described in Fonseca and Toscano 'Fostering teenagers' willingness to learn a foreign language' in Rubio, F. (ed), *Self-Esteem and Foreign Language Learning,* 2007 (Cambridge Scholars Publishing).

CHAPTER 2
A SENSE OF IDENTITY

Don Quixote to Sancho Panza:
'You must keep in view what you are,
striving to know yourself,
the most difficult thing to know that the mind can imagine.'

Miguel de Cervantes *Don Quixote de la Mancha*

Chapter 2: A Sense of Identity

A sense of identity refers to the knowledge and perceptions that we have of ourself. It is knowing who I am and what I can become. Identity can be described as the picture that one holds of oneself; and self-esteem is how we feel about that image.

Knowing who I am involves knowing and accepting both my light and my shadow. It means I have an accurate notion of my gifts, talents and abilities, including things I may take for granted, and it also includes recognising and accepting areas that still need to be developed, aspects that are in a state of potentiality.

Our potential, waiting in the shadow to grow, is often ignored. In *Hamlet*, Shakespeare wrote, 'we know what we are, but know not what we may be'. For our students, their areas of potential still to be developed will in part be language skills, but also there may be emotional intelligence factors of an interpersonal or intrapersonal nature which can greatly influence the language learning process.

Students that have a realistic vision of their abilities and their 'points for development' are more likely to place themselves in situations where there are greater possibilities of success and to avoid situations where they are likely to fail. They can accept criticism or comments related to their 'points for development', because they are already aware of them. And they don't necessarily 'buy' negative comments from others, because they are aware of their strengths, they know how to use them and they have the hope of improving in other areas.

Since students behave in ways that reflect their sense of identity, it is important for teachers to help them build a good self-image and to pay attention to their strengths so that they can see themselves in a positive way. This does not mean that we only recognise the positive. Students need to have a realistic appreciation of both their strengths and their current limitations in order to develop their strengths further and to work to towards reducing their limitations.

Regarding their language learning, it is necessary, of course, to make them aware of gaps in their knowledge. They need to know what to work on, but if they see themselves as co-creators of their learning, as holders of some control over the outcomes, they will take a more active role in the learning process, and this will lead to greater improvement.

If in the classroom we listen not only for the mistakes students make, but also really listen to the person behind the words, this can help to create a class committed to achievement. In such an atmosphere, mistakes are an integral and necessary part of learning. The way we deal with mistakes can definitely touch students' identity. A mistake can be a window to improve the student's interlanguage (their own version of the L2 which they speak as they learn), or it can be a reinforcement of a student's feeling that he or she is 'no good'. It all depends on how the mistake is dealt with (See also **My Mistake**, Activity 1.9).

The Sense of Identity
refers to the knowledge I have of myself.
It is knowing who I am and who I can become.

Teachers who promote a sense of identity:
- celebrate the uniqueness of individuals
- promote the development of a positive self-concept
- show acceptance of students, and interest in them as people
- help students recognise their strengths and their points to be developed.

Suggestions for Building a Sense of Identity

☐ In multicultural contexts, encourage students to identify with their cultural heritage by developing a class chart of traditions, special holidays, customs, traditional foods, values and contributions of different cultures and nationalities. Ask students to interview their parents, grandparents or other relatives to gather background information on their family history and traditions.

☐ Have students recognise their individual uniqueness by doing activities related to things such as voice, handwriting, or fingerprints.

☐ Begin a compliment chain by giving one student a genuine compliment, and asking that student to receive it as a gift from you. Have that student give another student a compliment, and so on, so that every student gains practice in giving and receiving a genuine compliment. This can be done in a circle where each person gives a compliment to the student to their right, so everyone gets to give and receive a compliment.

☐ Develop with the class as many ways as they can think of to give sincere praise or recognition to individuals, in verbal and non-verbal ways. Encourage them to use these when appropriate.

☐ For primary students, trace the outline of each student on a large piece of paper. Have students draw their own face and clothing, and label the main parts of the body and clothing in English. Post a different student portrait every week on the classroom door, and have class members suggest positive words or phrases that describe the featured student. Write their comments on the drawing, and allow students to take their portraits home.

☐ Have students cut out magazine pictures and create a collage that would tell others about things like their interests, favourite food, places they would like to visit, and favourite books and films. Post them in the room and have students look at them all to find things they have in common with others.

- When correcting papers, use a yellow highlighter to indicate to students the words or expressions that were used well, so students become more aware of their strengths in the language.

- Use a variety of words to make comments on students' papers, to show the positive features as well as the points for development.

- When possible, work with each student and encourage them to decide which language learning tasks are especially difficult for them and which are easy. Then discuss with them which ways they can deal with the tasks that are difficult for them.

- Encourage students to keep a daily diary or journal; they can include in it their thoughts for the day, their feelings about themselves, the things they worked hardest on, the things they learned. Ask them to hand in their diaries or journals on a periodic basis so you can gain greater insights into your students and provide them with supportive comments. These diaries would not be kept for grades, but for language practice and for helping them to understand themselves better.

- For students to be supported by their strengths, plan opportunities for them to display their unique talents or interests through classroom displays, performances or talent shows.

- Give students the opportunity to use puppets to represent experiences and problematic situations that they might be facing. Role play through puppets can be much less threatening.

- Provide opportunities for students to exercise leadership and responsibility.

- Find ways of conveying to each student that you really care about him or her as an individual.

- Provide opportunities and activities for students to share their personal thoughts, their feelings, their concerns in an atmosphere of acceptance (see **Circle Time**, Activity 2.5)

Teachers can help students modify their **self-concept**. In order to do this, it is necessary to focus systematically on the following:
- honouring individual uniqueness, building an awareness of unique qualities.
- contributing to positive self-images.
- demonstrating care and acceptance, creating an environment where all students feel they can be themselves.
- reinforcing more accurate self-descriptions.

2.1 We bingo

Focus: Interrogatives. Writing and speaking. This is an effective icebreaker that can help the students get to know more about each other's talents; they get practice asking and answering questions and using different verb tenses in a climate of having fun. This activity is recommended for the first weeks of the school year.

Level: Elementary +

Time: Lesson 1: 5-10 minutes; Lesson 2, 20-30 minutes

Preparation: Make photocopies of the questionnaire for each student.

in class

Lesson 1

1. Have your students fill in the following questionnaire, or prepare one that would be appropriate for their age and level. Give lower levels special help with the language they need. It can be very useful to know specific things about your students, to be able to relate to them on a more personal level, and the questionnaire can be saved for preparing other activities.

Name _____

1. When I have free time I like doing/making/going ...

2. Some interesting things I have done

3. Some things I know how to do

4. Something special I have

5. Some things I really like

6. Something I did last year

CHAPTER 2: A SENSE OF IDENTITY

2.1 We bingo

2. Collect the completed questionnaires, and for each question ask one or two students to say what they answered (*In my free time I go out with my friends ...*). With some, you can ask how many other students do the same. Then save these questionnaires in order to use the information to create a bingo card like the one below, with items personalised for your students. Try to include something from every student; but if you have over 24 students, select categories to be shared by more than one student. You can choose items which allow them to practise different verb tenses or vocabulary they have worked with.

Lesson 2

3. Before doing the activity, you may wish to practise the questions your students will need. If so, with the bingo card in hand, model some of the questions for them, and also give them a few minutes to think of the rest by themselves; then check with the whole class, until you are sure that they know how to formulate all the questions. For lower-level students, you may want to write some model questions on the board so they can use them while playing the game.

   For the sample bingo card below, some examples of questions are:
   Do you like chocolate?
   Do you love singing?
   Can you ride a horse?
   Do you speak two foreign languages?
   Are you computer smart?
   Do you own a bike?
   Are you well organised?
   Have you acted in a play?
   Have you ever won a prize?
   Have you walked along the beach at night?
   Have you been to another country?

4. Tell the students to talk to as many of their classmates as possible within the next few minutes in order 'to find someone who' for each category. When they do so, they write the person's name in the corresponding category. Before starting, tell them that the first person to complete the worksheet says *BINGO!* When someone has done this, tell that student to stand at the front, and allow a few more minutes, until two or three more have finished. Ask them to come to the front, too. Then say 'Game Over', and invite the rest of the class to sit down.

5. The next step is to start asking questions to the students at the front, for instance:
   Teacher: *Who likes chocolate?*
   Student 1 (from the information she has on her worksheet): *Silvia does.* (As you can imagine, all eyes will now go to Silvia.)

2.1 We bingo

Teacher to the rest of the 'winners' at the front: *Who else likes chocolate?* More names are said aloud, and this way, more students get attention from their classmates.

Continue this way, with two or three more categories, and then have the rest of the class ask their classmates at the front the remaining 'Who…?' questions.

is a good cook	reads a lot	plays football	owns a bike
has organised a party	can ride a horse	is computer smart	likes chocolate
has won a prize	has spoken in public	loves singing	does volunteer work
can speak two foreign languages	has taken part in a play	has eaten oysters	has been to another country
owns a bike	has planted a tree	is fond of music	can play an instrument
has walked along the beach at night	has gone sailing	is well-organised	has been to a zoo

2.2 Student of the week

Focus: To help students gain a deeper knowledge of themselves and of their classmates, and to practise asking and answering questions. It is best to use this activity when an accepting, friendly classroom atmosphere has been created.

Level: Lower intermediate +

Time: 20–30 minutes once a week

Preparation: Put the names of all your students inside a box that you keep, and once a week draw one name out of the box to select the Student of the Week.
If possible, bring a camera into the classroom.

in class

1. Ask the class, apart from the Student of the Week, to divide into groups of 4 or 5, and tell them to brainstorm things they would like to know about the chosen student. Ask them to write at least three questions. Moving from group to group, you can help them to polish the questions if necessary. In the meantime, tell the Student of the Week to use the time to jot down some ideas about something that he/she would like to share about himself/herself with the rest of the class. Make it clear that the Student of the Week may choose to answer all the questions or, for any of the questions, say 'I pass'.

2. Each group appoints a secretary to write down the final questions, and then decides who is going to ask them. Tell them to ask the questions as if they were interviewing a very important person; the secretary writes down the student's answers. After all the questions have been asked, in each group the students write a short paragraph to hand in about the student, incorporating the answers to their questions.

3. If you have a camera, take a picture of the student of the week while he or she is being interviewed. It can be used later on to make a Student of the Week poster, with his or her name, the photo and the answers to the questions. Space permitting, you might like to use a whole wall to put up all the Student of the Week posters as they are completed.
Questions can be similar to the ones used for **Question of the Day** (Activity 1.1.C). Here are other suggestions that can be used according to age, interests and language level:
   What is your favourite colour?
   Do you like sports?
   What is your favourite TV programme?
   What is your favourite part of the house?
   What changes would you like to make to your room?

2.2 Student of the week

What do you like most about school?
What do you like least about school?
How do you feel right now, about this interview?
What is your idea of a perfect day?
What is your idea of a perfect world?
What is the nicest thing that has ever happened to you?
What do you do when you get bored?
If you had Aladdin's lamp, what would you like to ask for?

Variation
In Step 1, while the groups are thinking of questions to ask, the Student of the Week can write on the blackboard or interactive whiteboard a few words about some of the things he or she would like to share. As these are seen by the students, the groups may get more ideas for questions.

Note
Be sure that everyone has a chance to be Student of the Week at some time. If there aren't enough weeks to include all students, you can have two Students of the Week.

2.3 True and false

Focus: Writing and speaking. Learning about each other in an atmosphere of play.

Level: Elementary +

Time: 15–20 minutes

Preparation: Think of three true statements about yourself, and one false.

in class

1. Tell students that they are going to write down four sentences about themselves, three true and one false. The true ones should be things that most of the class wouldn't already know – and should be things that they are happy to discuss in class – and the one that is false should be a reasonable option. To illustrate this, read your own statements aloud. Ask students to talk to the person next to them and decide which one is false. Call on one or two to see what they say and then tell them if they were right.

2. Put them in groups of 4 or 5 and have them write their sentences. In turn, they will read them aloud to the rest of their group, who will decide which they think are false.

3. If you have time left, you can ask one or two people from each group to tell the whole class something they have learned about someone in their group.

Note
This activity is good to do at the beginning of the course, because it helps students learn things about each other. As they can choose what they write, they only have to disclose information about themselves that they want to share, and so it is a very low-risk activity. The activity could be repeated another day.
It can also be a good way for students to get to know you. Jane usually starts her first class each year by writing on the blackboard either words that are somehow related to her life for students to try to guess what they mean, or true/false sentences about herself for students to say which they think are true.

Acknowledgement
We saw the idea of true/false sentences used in an activity for students in Puchta and Rinvolucri's *Multiple Intelligences in EFL,* 2005) Helbling Languages.

2.4 Talking about me

Focus: Speaking. We reinforce our sense of identity when we remember positive things about ourselves, and even more when we talk about them to others. One comfortable way to do this is in the context of a game.

Level: Lower intermediate +

Time: 30-40 minutes

Preparation: Bring a copy of the board (below) and a dice for each group.

in class

1. Put students randomly into groups of 3 or 4: have them sit in a circle in their group. Give each group a dice and a photocopy of the board. Then let them have a few minutes to read the things they may have to talk about and to get some ideas. At this time they can use dictionaries or ask you how to say anything they are not sure about.

2. Each group member throws the dice and the student with the highest number begins the game. Each time, a student throws the dice, moves the number of squares shown on the dice, and then talks for 30 to 60 seconds about what is indicated on the square they have landed on. The first student to reach FINISH is the winner, but in this game everyone wins because they are all benefiting from the positive atmosphere established.

START ➡	One person who has helped me	One thing I would like to learn	One thing I can do well	How I am feeling today ⬇
A nice experience I have had this week ⬇	A goal I have	Something that makes me happy	Someone that I admire	A time I helped someone ⬅
A value that is important for me ➡	A friend	Something I am grateful for	An object in my home that is special for me	A place that is special for me ⬇
A word I really like in English ⬇	A pleasant memory	Something I learned this week	My favourite song	A time someone helped me ⬅
Someone in my family ➡	One thing I hope to do during the next year	A time I was surprised	A nice present I received	FINISH

CHAPTER 2: A SENSE OF IDENTITY

2.4 Talking about me

A shorter version of the game can be played using a coin. With heads, students move one space, with tails, two.

START ➡	One person who has helped me	One thing I would like to learn	One thing I can do well	How I am feeling today ⬇
A nice experience I have had this week ⬇	A goal I have	Something that makes me happy	Someone that I admire	A time I helped someone ⬅
A value that is important for me ➡	A friend	A time someone helped me	Something I am grateful for	FINISH

Extension
After all groups have finished, and still in their circles, each student says to the whole class one thing that he or she has learned about a classmate during the game. So that everyone will be mentioned, you can specify that the students select something about the student on their left.

2.5 Circle time

Focus: Speaking, listening and writing. This is a group activity that uses strategies aimed at helping students develop skills to understand themselves and express their individuality.

Level: Elementary +

Time: 30–50 minutes, depending on material selected.

Preparation: Choose a story, poem, speech, letter, short video or any other material in the target language that would be appropriate for your students. It should illustrate some theme you would like to deal with in class. For example, fear, courage, friendship ...

in class

1. Have your students read, listen to or watch the material you have prepared. Do any work on the text that you would normally do, such as explain new words first, or answer questions or discuss afterwards.

2. Have students sit in a circle. Be part of the circle too, and say an incomplete sentence which relates in some way to the work done previously. ('I'm good at ...', 'I feel angry when ...', 'A friend is ...').

3. Go around the circle, and each student completes the sentence. You can pass a small ball or some other object if you wish for the person speaking to hold.

4. The first time you do Circle Time you need to make clear the rules of the game:
   - Talk only when it is your turn, and only to complete the sentence.
   - Listen respectfully to others.
   - You can say 'I pass' if you wish.
   - You can use your mother tongue if you need to.

   If lower level students do use their L1, you can translate their completion in a soft voice. If learners make mistakes that may hinder comprehension or mistakes related to a teaching point you are dealing with, you can correct them indirectly by reformulating quietly what they said wrong in a correct way, (Student: 'A friend is someone which helps you.' You: 'Yes, a friend is someone who helps you.') The important thing is not to interrupt the flow.

5. Take notes of their completions, including any new language needed. If you wish, you can make a mind map (see end of activity) of their completions on a flip chart or on an interactive whiteboard to keep for the students to review the language after everyone has finished.
   As you write your notes, make any corrections needed – but don't

2.5 Circle time

treat this as grammar study. You can leave the flip chart up for students to see, or if you have written the mind map on an interactive whiteboard and saved it to the computer, you can show it another day for a quick review.

Variation
Secret thoughts: you can choose sentence stems you think your students might be interested in but not find it easy to talk about openly ('I feel jealous when…' or 'Something that really bothers me is …'). They complete the sentences in writing on a slip of paper, adding more details if they wish, but **not** putting their name to it. Pick these up and put them in a box. The students each draw one out of the box and read a secret thought. If any authors want to disclose their identity they can raise their hands when theirs is read, but stress that this is not necessary. With a well-functioning group you might then also ask questions to the group: *Can anyone else add anything about when they feel jealous?* or *Does anyone have a suggestion about what to do when you are angry?*

Notes
1. Circle Time is an activity that becomes more effective for language learning the more it is repeated. With lower levels especially, it is very helpful for students to see things that they have said appearing on the mind map, as this makes the language very memorable. The first time you do Circle Time, students may be more reticent to speak up and many may pass, but as the group becomes more connected throughout the course and students become more confident, we have found that they become very enthused with this activity and they assimilate a lot of language.

2. In her research project with children in Argentina (de Andrés 1999:93–4), Verónica found that Circle Time was 'an invaluable tool for the development of speaking and listening skills: from our observations it was noted that listening to each other gradually became part of the normal attitude and speech was significantly improved'. She found that near 'the end of the ten-week programme most children were expressing themselves in English, with little use of the mother tongue' and she also noted that it was a good way 'for shy children to express themselves and be heard. Even in a foreign language!'

2.5 Circle time

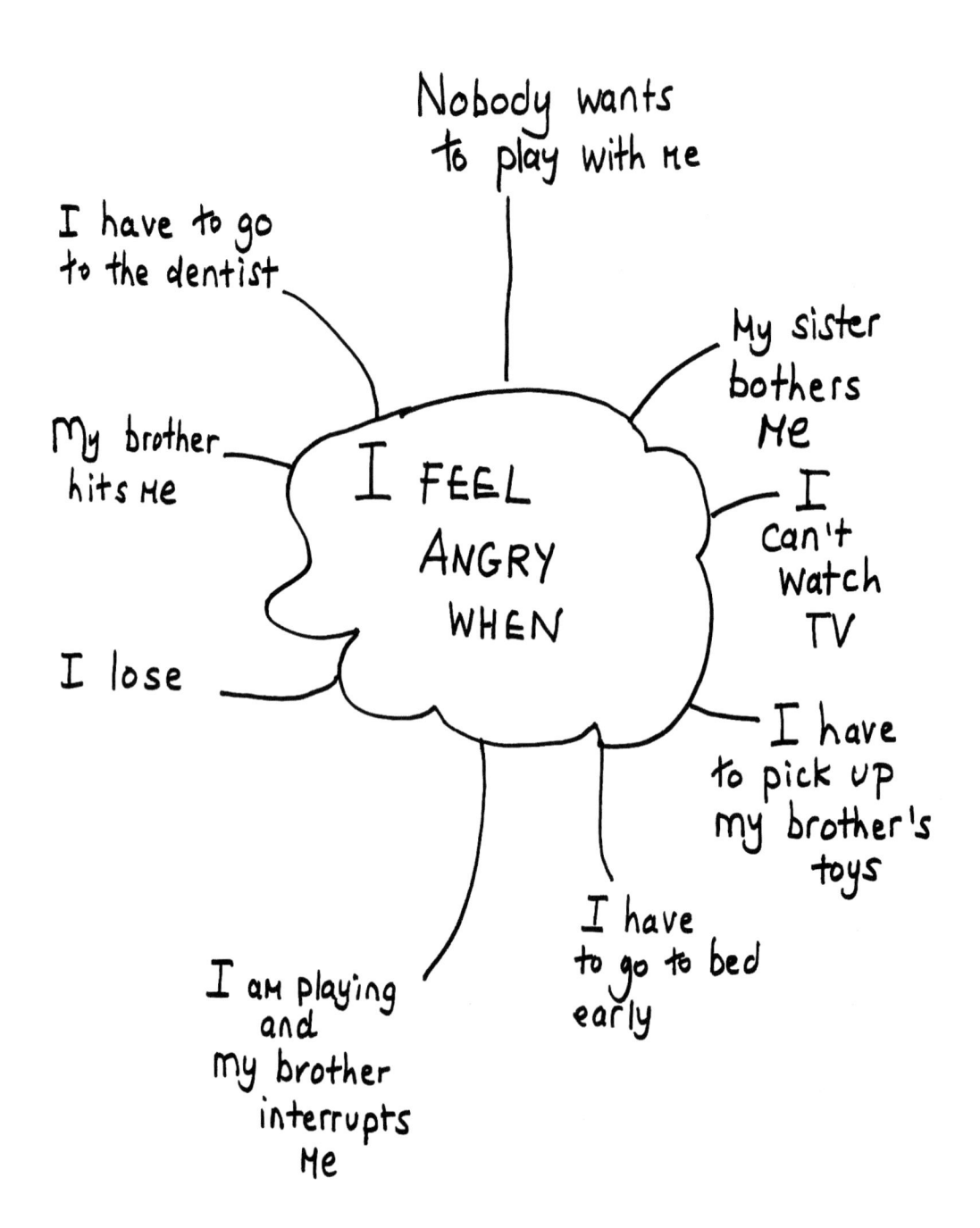

I FEEL ANGRY WHEN

- Nobody wants to play with me
- I have to go to the dentist
- My sister bothers me
- My brother hits me
- I can't watch TV
- I lose
- I have to pick up my brother's toys
- I have to go to bed early
- I am playing and my brother interrupts me

2.6 Be yourself

Focus: Reading and speaking.

Level: Lower intermediate +

Time: 40–50 minutes

Preparation: Have the presentation on the CD of the video with the poem by Fritz Perls (below) ready to project from your computer, or bring in a CD player and some soft background music. Print a copy of the poem for each student.

in class

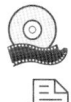

1. Present the video version of the poem on the CD, or alternatively read it aloud, playing your music. If you read the poem aloud, be sure to respect the rhythm of the music.

2. Review vocabulary if necessary. Hand out the printed copies.

3. If using the CD, show the video again and ask your students to repeat it to themselves as it appears. Otherwise, have them read the printed poem to themselves.

4. Students read it a third time to themselves, underlining their favourite word or line.

5. Tell them now, to stand up and do a milling exercise, i.e. walking around the classroom, greeting as many people as possible; every time they meet with somebody they say aloud their favourite word or line to each other.

6. After a few moments, ask them to get together with classmates who have chosen the same line or word and discuss why they chose that line or word. Allow time for interaction. If some students don't have a group, have them all form another group and agree on a word or line they all like.

7. Next, ask them to create something new, using the key idea or thought that came out of that word or line, e.g. a drawing, a poster, a new poem, story or song.

8. Each group presents their work.

2.6 Be yourself

> Be as you are
> And so see who you are
> And how you are
> Let go for a moment or two
> Of what you ought to do
> And discover what you do do
> Risk a little if you can
> Feel your own feelings
> Say your own words
> Think your own thoughts
> Be your own self
> Discover
> Let the plan for you
> Grow from within you.
>
> **Fritz Perls**

Notes

1. This inspiring poem by Fritz Perls, the founder of Gestalt Therapy, can be used as a tool to affirm who we are – and, more importantly, to discover who we can be.

2. It may be necessary to use more than one lesson for students to complete the final presentation.

2.7 A commercial about yourself

Focus: Writing. To help students think more positively about themselves, and give them the chance to get to know each other better.

Level: Lower intermediate +

Time: 40–50 minutes

Preparation: For Variation 1, a variety of magazines, some scissors and big sheets of paper/card to make a collage.

in class

1. Tell your students to imagine that they are going to participate in a job selection interview, and this activity will be a way of helping them to get ready. They are going to need to create a poster or an advertisement about themselves, describing the positive qualities that they can offer.

2. To start their commercial, they will need to complete the statement: I am _____, followed by at least seven adjectives or short phrases. Then they will need to write a few more lines about themselves. (If you see any students having difficulty with this, pair them and ask them to describe their partner.) You can give them a few ideas, adapted according to the interests and level of your students:
   - Something you like about yourself is ...
   - You do your best when ...
   - How would others describe you?
   - What is your favourite colour, music, book, TV programme?
   - Which fictional hero or heroine do you feel most identified with?
   - If you could make three wishes, what would they be?
   - If you had a magic carpet, what places would you like to visit?
   - What is something that you think might be good for others to know about you?

3. Once the students have finished writing their commercial, invite them to come to the front one at a time to read it for the class and receive a round of applause.

Variations

1. Students can create posters by cutting out magazine images and words that best describe them, and making a collage with these. The posters can be later displayed on a special notice board.

2. If you have an interactive whiteboard to use, as a little project get your students to prepare their commercial at home, finding interesting pictures on the internet to add to it. They can send

2.7 A commercial about yourself

you these by email, and then each day you can have three to five students presenting their commercials in class. If you wish, they can be inserted within regular class work, as commercials are inserted into a television programme. Before each student begins their presentation, open the material they have sent to you on the screen of the interactive whiteboard.

2.8 A two-minute interview

Focus: To create a positive mood in the classroom by allowing students to communicate with each other in a personalised way. It is also good for practising listening skills, as well as asking and answering questions. By spending some time at the beginning of the course with activities like this, which focus on students sharing things closely linked to their identity, you will be establishing a classroom climate which facilitates learning the language. This is a good activity to do after **Listen to me** (Activity 1.7).

Level: Intermediate +

Time: 20 minutes

Preparation: Slips of paper and a box for Step 3.

in class

1. Tell your students they are going to interview each other. Some possibilities for questions are:
   - ☐ Something they did that was very successful.
   - ☐ A memorable learning experience.
   - ☐ A great trip.
   - ☐ A favourite hobby.
   - ☐ A person who loves you (why do they love you?).
   - ☐ A person you love (why do you love them?).
   - ☐ A scary moment.
   - ☐ A person you admire.
   - ☐ Something that makes you feel happy.
   - ☐ A place you would like to visit.
   - ☐ A dream you would like to have come true.
   - ☐ A house you would like to have.

   Encourage your students to add to the list of possible topics. Suggest they include things that they would like to talk about. If they have options that they are really interested in, it will be easier for them to open up and express themselves.

2. You may want to practise with your students how to ask questions about some of the topics selected. Give them a few minutes to think of and write down the questions they want to ask their partner. You can provide any help they need with the language. They can choose to ask as many questions they want. Often, students will choose to ask one question about several topics, but they may also decide to ask a number of questions which explore one or two topics in more depth.

3. To put students in pairs, have half the class write their name on a little piece of paper and put it in a box. The other half draws a name out to see who will be their partner. In case there is an odd number of students, be ready to take part yourself.

2.8 A two-minute interview

4. Tell them that A will ask B questions during one minute, and B will listen without interrupting. Stop them when the minute is over, and tell them that after this, B will take one minute to reply to the questions that B wants to answer. When this minute is over, switch roles.

   They can be reminded that an important part of the activity is learning to listen actively, B to the questions their partner asks them and A to the answers their partner gives to their questions.

Variation

An alternative question-and-answer activity, very closely connected with identity, is the following:

In pairs, A asks B the question 'Who are you?' When B answers, maybe with his/her name or other general information, A repeats the same question. This continues for a total of ten repetitions. Then B asks A the same question ten times. For lower levels, you may want to be sure they know the construction 'I am a person who ...' before beginning.

As a follow-up, ask learners to write a paragraph describing themselves based on, though not necessarily repeating, the answers they gave to the ten questions.

2.9 Magic combs

Focus: This activity is very useful for learning and practising adjectives of personal description. It is aimed at helping students gain a sense of self-worth. We know that what we focus on is what we get, so by doing this activity your students will be more aware of their good qualities and will be more likely to show them in and out of the classroom.

Level: Lower intermediate +

Time: 20-30 minutes

Preparation: For Variation 1, coloured paper.

in class

1. Begin the activity by writing your given name on the blackboard vertically (like a down answer in a crossword), as in the examples below:

   ```
   A        M
   L        A
   V        R
   A        I
   R        E
   O
   ```

   Then tell your students that we all have many positive qualities – some that are highly developed, and others that we still need to work on. Ask the students to help you find positive qualities that begin with each letter of your name; have a short brainstorming session with them for each letter, and one at a time choose an adjective for each, the adjectives that you feel best describe you. When you finish, draw some lines around the words, in the shape of a comb (see below), and tell them that this is a magic comb – it is magic because you can use it to clean your head from negative thoughts about yourself.

2. When you have finished modelling the activity, tell your students to do the same: to write their names on a piece of paper, in a vertical way, and think of positive qualities they have, and write one which begins with each letter of their name. Tell them that if they get stuck, they can ask their classmates to help them find the adjectives, focusing on qualities they see. This is a very good way to raise your students' awareness of their own good points and also to get them know more about what others see in them. You can also tell them that they can look for words using the dictionary; you will be surprised at their willingness to search for words!

2.9 Magic combs

```
Active
Loyal
Versatile
Appreciative
Responsible
Optimistic
```

```
Modern
Artistic
Reliable
Idealistic
Enthusiastic
```

Variations
1. You might want to bring in coloured paper for them to make the magic combs on, and then put them up around the room.

2. You can have students work in pairs and think of words for half the letters of their names, and then have their partner think of the remaining words.

2.10 The talking stick

Focus: The aim of this activity is to encourage students to identify their cultural and/or family heritage, and feel proud of it by sharing this information with the rest of the class. This activity can be a bridge to their new world for students that come to your country from different cultural backgrounds, since by creating a safe place for disclosure of aspects of their identity, we are giving them the message that we can expand our cultural awareness, we can celebrate our differences, and we can develop mutual understanding. In short, we can grow by learning from each other.

Level: Intermediate +

Time: Lesson 1: 20–30 minutes
Lesson 2: depends on the size of the class
For the variations: another class period

Preparation: For Lesson 2, bring in a CD player to play the Native American music on Track 2 of the CD or something similar of your choice, plus an interesting object of your own, and one or more interesting sticks about 30 cm (1 ft) long (see Step 4).
For the extension, photocopies of the text and the medicine wheel.

in class

Lesson 1

1. Tell your students to bring to class for a future lesson (set a date) a special object that represents something linked to a family or cultural tradition. It can be something related to their customs or traditional foods, and even to their family or cultural values. If they don't have an actual object to bring in, they can bring a photo of it, or make a drawing of it.

2. Discuss with your students the purpose of the activity: tell them to think of something they would like to share with the rest of the class about themselves, their culture or their family, and to think of an object that can hold that 'story'.

3. Tell them that they are now going to prepare a short speech, about 3–5 minutes, about the object. If your class is large, ask your students to prepare shorter speeches, or use two class periods. Give your students some class time to prepare this presentation. Offer your help during this preparation stage.

Lesson 2

4. The day of the Show and Tell activity, ask your students to sit in a circle. Play the background music softly, to create a special warm atmosphere. Present your stick, or several if you have decided to do the activity in small groups.

2.10 The talking stick

5. Tell them you will be using the Talking Stick, a technique for communication based on the traditional Native American way of allowing everyone to express themselves during a tribal meeting. According to this tradition, the stick has special qualities that call the spirit of the ancestors to guide the participants when making decisions; for us the great value of this technique is that using the stick ensures that everyone has the right to speak, and the circle – the shape of harmony – stands for equal value of all the opinions expressed.

6. The guidelines for using the Talking Stick are as follows:
   - Give the Talking Stick to one student. Only that student has the right to speak; only that student has 'the power of the words'.
   - The rest of the class must remain silent.
   - The student will show the object he or she has brought into the class and will tell the story behind the object in no more than 5 minutes.
   - The rest of the class is asked to listen without commenting. This creates a feeling of a mutual caring and respect that allows the activity to flow.
   - When the student holding the stick finishes, the stick is passed to the student next to him or her. Alternatively, the stick can be put in the middle of the circle and when a student is ready to speak, they take the stick and begin.
   - Students will speak only when they have the Talking Stick. You can do this at the beginning, to model the activity for the rest of the class, telling them about your object. At the end you can also use the Stick to ask for feedback about the activity.

Note
Lesson 2 can be done as a whole-class activity or in small groups. Decide how to do it according to the time available and also the atmosphere you want to create. The advantage of doing it in small groups is the greater feeling of intimacy, whereas doing it as a whole-class activity requires more time but allows more extensive interaction and stronger bonding of the whole class.

Variation
Before having students sit in the circle, have them stand in a square and ask how they feel. Does everyone feel equal? Do they feel connected equally to all their classmates? Are there positions of greater or lesser importance? Then have them move into a circle and compare how they feel then.

Extension
1. Ask students to read the following text from *Black Elk Speaks*. Then they are to prepare something that this passage suggests to them, to present in the following class. Some suggestions would be:

2.10 The talking stick

- a drawing
- a simple poem
- a list of other things in nature that are circular
- the information from the passage, in the form of an interview with Black Elk
- a composition: Circles and squares in my life
- a dialogue between a circle and a square.

In the second lesson, each person presents what they did.

> I came to live here where I am now between Wounded Knee Creek and Grass Creek. Others came too, and we made these little gray houses of logs that you see, and they are square. It is a bad way to live, for there can be no power in a square. You have noticed that everything an Indian does is in a circle, and that is because the Power of the world always works in circles, and everything tries to be round. In the old days when we were a strong and happy people, all our power came to us from the sacred hoop of the nation, as so long as the hoop was unbroken, the people flourished. The flowering tree was the living center of the hoop, and the circle of the four quarters nourished it. The east gave peace and light, the south gave warmth, the west gave rain, and the north with its cold and mighty wind gave strength and endurance ... The sky is round, and I have heard that the earth is round, like a ball, and so are all the stars. The wind, in its greatest power, whirls. Birds make their nests in circles, for theirs is the same religion as ours. The sun comes forth and goes down again in a circle. The moon does the same, and both are round. Even the seasons form a great circle in their changing, and always come back again to where they were. The life of a man is a circle from childhood to childhood, and so it is in everything where power moves. Our tepees were round like the nests of birds, and these were always set in a circle, the nation's hoop, a nest of many nests, where the Great Spirit meant for us to hatch our children.
> But the Wasichus (white men) have put us in these square boxes. Our power is gone and we are dying, for the power is not in us any more.
>
> Neihardt, J. 2008. *Black Elk Speaks*. SUNY Press.

2. Optional: each student makes their own medicine wheel. This is a tool used by the native American tribes to help people to understand themselves and reach their potential. Originally, medicine wheels were made with stones in the wilderness, but today other forms are also used; this activity is a free adaptation.

2.10 The talking stick

You can explain that each part of the wheel represents one of the directions of the compass as well as an aspect of the person. Give each student a copy of the wheel, and have them decide on words or drawings to put in each concentric circle, according to the scheme below. These can be ones they would associate with the aspect in that part of the wheel.

a = animal
b = symbol
c = qualities and values
d = dreams

This can be done as a short exercise in class, or it can be assigned as a project to be done at home, with greater reflection and elaboration.

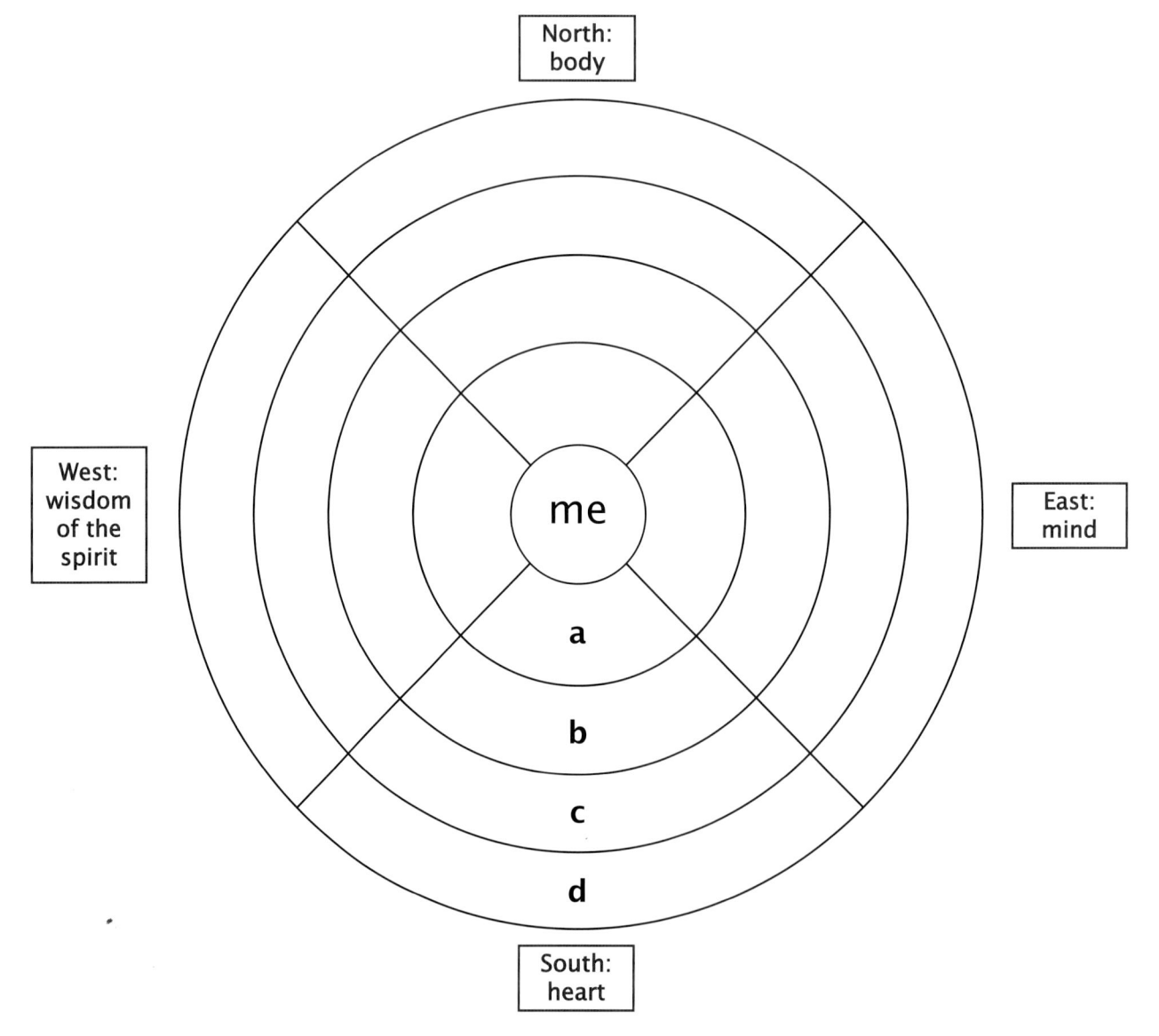

North: body

West: wisdom of the spirit

me

East: mind

a
b
c
d

South: heart

CHAPTER 2: A SENSE OF IDENTITY

2.11 Who are you three?

Focus: This exercise is meant to help your students enhance their self-image. Our self-image directs our behaviour and permeates all the choices we make, and has a very significant impact on learning. Therefore, if students improve their self-image, it is likely that at the same time they will improve their overall performance. From the language learning perspective, this activity will provide them with the opportunity to learn meaningful vocabulary and to make accurate personal descriptions.

Level: Intermediate +

Time: 30 minutes (50 with follow-up)

Preparation: A photocopy of the worksheet for each student.

in class

1. Explain to your students that we have three selves:
   - ☐ the actual self, which is a picture of how you see yourself in the many different roles which are part of your self-image (for students, their self-images as learners and friends are often the most important ones).
   - ☐ the ideal self, which is basically about how you would like to see yourself, who you want to become.
   - ☐ the public self, which is the image you want to show to others.

   You might want to tell your students that when these three pictures are not in harmony, we are out of balance and we don't work and learn as effectively as we might. Tell your students that the purpose of this exercise is to raise their awareness of these *three selves* in order to create a better learning state.

2. Next, brainstorm with the whole class the words and expressions that may be necessary for accurate self-descriptions. Write these on the board. Then give students the following worksheet, they are to complete it, and then share with a partner whatever they would like. A whole-class discussion could follow.

2.11 Who are you three?

MY THREE SELVES
My actual self – how I see myself in my many roles (student/teacher, friend …)   _____   (four words that describe how you see yourself)
My ideal self – how I would like to become: _____   (four words that describe how you would **like** to see yourself)
My public self – how I like others to see me: _____   (four words others could use to describe you)
Questions to think about: 1. What do the three selves have in common?   2. How do they differ?   3. What can you do to move closer to your ideal self?

Extension (for upper intermediate to advanced students)
Some possible questions for written reflection would be the following:

1. Which is more important; the way you feel about yourself, or the way others see you?

2. How can feeling good about yourself affect your performance?

3. How does your self-image (as a student/friend/family member) affect your life?

4. What can you do to feel good about yourself?

5. Remember a time when you really felt good about yourself. Bring back all the details. What did you do that made you feel good? Who was with you? Where were you? How could you feel that way again?

CHAPTER 3
A SENSE OF BELONGING

> Do you know where self esteem comes from? It comes from our peers, from being liked, accepted and connected.
>
> David Johnson

Chapter 3: A Sense of Belonging

In addition to having a strong sense of identity, for healthy self-esteem we also need a feeling of being accepted and being connected, especially with the people we consider important in our life. We need to belong. Much research shows that people with healthy relationships have fewer serious problems and live longer. This also has a direct impact on the brain and learning. Our brain is a social brain. To learn effectively, we need to connect to others.

Teachers can contribute to increasing a sense of belonging in the classroom and enhancing the general atmosphere of the school. A sense of belonging is especially important for adolescent students, because to be able to feel good about themselves they also need to feel a part of something larger than themselves – a family, a team, a culture, a community – that they feel proud of. Some students may have nothing they are proud to feel part of, and it is teachers who can create this space for them; a classroom where respect and concern for others exist can provide an important source of community for young people.

You as a teacher can do a great deal in order to facilitate social acceptance. To achieve this, you can explore ways to establish a supportive classroom atmosphere – a place which students are happy to belong to. You could do this, for example, by showing your own positive attitude towards the group, by encouraging peer approval and support among students, and by letting every student know they have a place in the group. It is also very useful to provide opportunities for the group to share moments both of significant effort and of achievement and to work on projects which are of service to others.

With language learning, the group is even more important, as interaction is an essential part of much of the learning process. Dörnyei and Murphey (2003:3-4) sum it up this way: 'In a 'good' group, the L2 classroom can turn out to be such a pleasant and inspiring environment that the time spent there is a constant source of success and satisfaction for teachers and learners alike. And even if someone's commitment should flag, his or her peers are likely to 'pull the person along' by providing the necessary motivation to persist'. They mention the TEAM acronym: Together Everyone Achieves More.

The Sense of Belonging
exists when we feel accepted in a group.

Teachers who promote a sense of belonging:
- create a climate of acceptance
- reduce the number of isolated students
- develop group identity
- promote a feeling of pride in the group
- support interpersonal relationships in the class.

Suggestions for Building a Sense of Belonging

- Make a chart including things such as birthdates, birthplaces, siblings, pets, favourite games, hobbies and interests. This can help students to find out what they have in common with others.

- Make a poster of new students that includes things such as the students' pictures, family information, birthdays, birthplaces, and latest places of residence. Place the poster inside or outside the classroom, so that everyone can get to know the new students and they can start to feel part of the group.

- Create a notice board with photos of each student to help them be identified. Play bingo with students' names, or play other games which encourage students to call each other by name.

- Ask students to bring a 'Me-Bag' with three to five objects that have a special meaning to them. Display them on an 'interest table' and have students take turns to speak about them, so everyone gets to know things about the rest of the group.

- Assign students to cooperative learning groups, so that they can bond with a small group of supportive students. In a foreign language class, it is easier at first to speak in a small group rather than in front of the whole class.

- Get each cooperative learning group to select a motto that best represents their philosophy or that highlights a thought or idea they feel is important. The motto could be put onto a poster they make about themselves.

- Put students in pairs for special activities that are to be completed outside the classroom (using the library, interviewing staff members to write up something about them in the target language ...)

- Encourage the cooperative learning groups or teams to discuss the characteristics of good team members and identify the traits they value most.

- Plan ways to celebrate birthdays: a song, an appreciation note or certificate, or other ways your class enjoys.

- Teach students non-competitive games, so that all students can participate and enjoy themselves without the pressure of competition.

- Observe students in your class to identify those who tend to be isolated. Keep records of their progress, and make a special effort to have these students sitting near others who will accept them or include them.

- Work individually with students who seem to need to develop social skills, to help them see the impact of their behaviour on others. Try to find ways to show them how to have more positive social relationships. For example, you might let them have special responsibilities in class where others will need their help in some way.

- Teach students who exhibit leadership skills how to deal with their classmates without dominating (leadership is basically about effective communication). Help them to understand students who have problems and to become aware of ways they can contribute to making it possible for these students to feel accepted.

- Build a sense of class and school pride by engaging in class service projects, helping to make your classroom or school look nice, planting a garden, or planning a party.

- Encourage students to use respectful behaviour toward each other, expressing thanks or appreciation for acts of kindness. You might have them do a role-play in the target language or create a puppet show with two different situations – one where someone is treated poorly and one where appreciation is shown – and have them discuss how they think the person felt.

> **Students with a sense of belonging can identify when it is important to act as individuals and when it is important to act as members of a team. It is students with a sense of belonging who can appreciate that they are different and unique, and that at the same time they share many basic qualities with their classmates.**

3.1 Mirroring

Focus: This activity can help students connect to each other and learn to take turns to lead and be led. From the language learning point of view, this activity can be used as a springboard to speak about feelings.

Level: Elementary +

Time: 10 minutes

Preparation: None.

in class

1. Ask the students to stand in two rows, facing each other. Numbers should be even; if not, be ready to participate yourself. They pair up with the person in front of them.
   Have the students in one row be the mirrors and the others the leaders or the 'doers', who move as they wish for their 'mirror' to imitate. Tell them that they can use the whole body, and they can make sounds too. Get them to find a space where they can move around, and begin. After a few minutes they change roles.

2. When both students in each pair have had a chance to be mirrors, invite them to sit down and discuss what happened to them. Beginners can use the L1. You can guide them with some questions such as:
   - How did you feel when doing the activity?
   - Which was it easier for you to be, the mirror or the leader?
   - How does this resemble what you do in life?

Variation
With students in the two rows, call on one student to begin to move, and the rest of the class mirrors his or her movements. After a while, call on another student to be the leader. Change several times. A very pleasant atmosphere is created when everyone is moving in harmony.

3.1 Mirroring

Note
With language teaching, we obviously want to provide a lot of linguistic input for our students. However, at certain moments a short non-verbal activity can be useful. The attention span of students, especially adolescents, is rather short; we may give a highly developed explanation of a topic, but if we don't have our students' attention, learning may not be going on. The mind appreciates a break now and then, and activities incorporating movement such as this one or **Back to Back** (Activity 3.2) help get more oxygen to the brain, and provide some productive downtime and a change of pace, after which students can get back to work and concentrate better.

3.2 Back to back

Focus: To develop bonding between students, and learn parts of the body.

Level: Elementary +

Time: 5 minutes

Preparation: Bring a CD player to play Track 3 of the CD or some rhythmic, spirited folk music.

in class

1. This is a good game for boosting energy. If you do this activity with elementary-level students, you can pre-teach vocabulary for the parts of the body, or use the activity when this lexical area is covered in the course material. With the music playing, tell your students to stand up and get a partner, and begin by standing back to back. Make sure that everyone has a partner, and be ready to play yourself if necessary.

2. Give fun commands for the students to follow with their partner, such as head-to-head, elbow-to-elbow or knee-to-knee. When you say 'All Change!', students get a new partner. This activity may be more effective with children and adults than with adolescents.

Variation
After you have given a number of commands, you can get different students to lead.

Acknowledgement
This is a version of an activity we learned from Eva Jonai.

3.3 Groups or pairs

Focus: To develop a good group climate in which students are able to express themselves freely and confidently. It is vital for students to get to know each other; if they always sit near to and work with the same classmates, it will be much more difficult to create this atmosphere. For this reason, it is useful to have a bank of techniques for dividing them up so that they work with as many other students as possible. Some of the possibilities are outlined below; see also **Signs of the Zodiac**, Activity 3.14.

Level: Elementary +

Time: 5–10 minutes for each option.

Preparation: For the second activity, bring in different coloured ribbons, each about 75 cm (3 ft) long, one for every two students in the class.

in class

- Groups: the most common way is to number them off. If you have 20 students and want them in groups of 4, give each student a number from one to five (4 × 5 = 20) and all the number ones meet in one part of the class, the twos in another, etc.

- Pairs: hold the ribbons in your hand so the ends hang free, and each student takes one end of a ribbon. The person on the other end of the ribbon will be their partner. For large classes, divide the ribbons and hold half of them in one hand, half in the other.

- Groups: if you don't need exactly equal groups, you can write on cards the name of several tourist destinations that you think would be interesting for your students, and put the cards up in different places around the room. Tell the students to go and stand by the name of the place they would most like to visit. If you have written, for example, Australia and you get a very large group there, be prepared to have a second option to get smaller groups (the beaches – the cities). The students could then discuss why they chose the destination as a quick warm-up before they do the main activity.

Note
See **Inspiring Quotations**, Activity 4.4, for suggestions using quotations.

3.4 Marching together

Focus: This activity is good for team-building and for working with following directions in the target language. For more advanced students, it can then be the basis for a speaking and writing activity.

Level: Elementary +

Time: 15 minutes

Preparation: Bring a CD player to play Track 4 of the CD or some other lively music that invites to you to move.

in class

1. Push desks back to leave as much free space as possible in the room. Begin the activity by playing the music. With students standing up, tell them, *Be interesting! Move different parts of the body! Get moving!* Then instruct them to form pairs shoulder to shoulder, and to start marching or walking around. While they do this, they decide on a word in the target language that they both like. After a few seconds, tell them to part and take five steps in any direction, and with their eyes closed find each other again by saying their word.

2. Then tell them to get into groups of 4 and, with all four shoulder to shoulder, to march or walk and again find a word they all like. Again, after a few moments, tell them to part, take five steps, and with their eyes closed find each other by saying their word.
For higher levels this can lead into a discussion of the topic of Team Building or Belonging. Have them work in their group of 4 to talk about the experience and draw conclusions. Each student in the group then writes one sentence about how they experienced this activity, and the group combines the four sentences into a statement or poem, making any small changes necessary. They then read these out to the rest of the class.

Note
If you have a large group and little space, explore the possibility of doing this activity outside on a nice day.

3.5 Line-ups

Focus: This is an activity that can be used at the beginning of the school year to help the members of a group get to know one another quickly. It can be used to teach months of the year; it can also be used for teaching comparatives and superlatives.

Level: Beginners +

Time: 5-15 minutes

Preparation: None.

in class

1. For lower levels, pre-teach the months of the year and how to say dates in English, then tell the students they are going to form a line according to their date of birth (January 9, March 13, April 23 …). Mark where January is in the room, and then have them quickly get into line according to their birthday. Then go down the line and get each of them to say aloud their name and their date of birth. If 'twins' get together, it is great fun!

2. With higher-level students you can then tell them that the ones that have a birthday in the same month should get together. If there are students that don't share a month with anyone else, get them into groups according to the season of the year in which their birthday falls. Have them discuss what they like or don't like about having a birthday at that time of the year. If you want to encourage them to speak more, they could each tell about a birthday they remember.

3. Other criteria to use for forming lines could be:
   - from the tallest to the shortest
   - the youngest to the oldest
   - the distance they live from the school.

   You can then call on them to make comparative/superlative sentences ('Carmen is taller than Ana.' 'Alexis is the tallest person in the class.')

Extension

Have students turn the line into a circle and each learn the name and one interesting thing about the person to their right. Then go around the circle with each student telling something about the classmate on his or her right.

3.6 Role-playing conflicts

Focus: This activity is good for conflict resolution and for developing speaking and writing skills in the target language.

Level: Lower intermediate +

Time: 40-50 minutes

Preparation: None.

in class

1. Have students form groups of 3 or 4; the task for each group is to identify a conflict existing in the class or an imaginary one that could exist in a classroom, and together they write the lines of a script for a role-play giving an example of the problem, *but not defining it or mentioning it explicitly*. A solution to the problem should be incorporated.

2. Then they will act it out, and the rest of the class can decide on a title for the role-play which will identify the issue (e.g. 'being rejected', 'not respecting others').

Variation
The groups can, as above, write and act out problem situations, but without including a solution. The class can offer possible suggestions and then they can act it out again, adding the solution they like best.

3.7 Take the weight off your shoulders

Focus: The aim of this exercise is to bring the group together at the end of a session, or when relaxation is needed; and it is also used to work with following directions in the target language.

Level: Elementary +

Time: 5–10 minutes

Preparation: Bring a CD player to play Track 5 on the CD or some other relaxing music. Alternatively, prepare to project something like the John Denver song 'Sunshine on my shoulders', which you can find on youtube.

in class

1. Play the music, and ask your students to stand up and form a circle. For a few minutes, give them some commands such as *Take a step into the circle, take a step to the right, raise your left hand ...*

2. After giving them several commands, tell them to stand in the circle and all face to their right, so that they're looking at their neighbour's back. Then ask them to put their left hand on the left shoulder of the person in front of them, and their right hand on that person's right shoulder. Tell them to start moving their fingers slowly and gently, with a pressure that feels comfortable. Now each person is giving and receiving a massage; and after a minute or two, ask them to turn around and continue giving and receiving the massage with a different partner.

Note
Touch is very important for healthy development, but before doing this – or indeed any activity that requires touch – be sure that it is appropriate and completely acceptable in your teaching context.

3.8 Blindfold walk

Focus: To build confidence and trust; also to experience the difference between leading and being led. To practise giving instructions.

Level: Lower intermediate +

Time: 20 minutes

Preparation: Bring material for blindfolds, enough for one per pair in your class.

in class

1. Have your students get into pairs and give each pair a blindfold. Ask them to decide who will be the leader first, and who will be the follower. Tell them the leaders will have a specified time (3–5 minutes is suggested) to guide their blindfolded partners on a walk. The leaders will have to describe to their followers what they need to do to avoid colliding into objects (e.g. 'turn to your left/right, walk two steps towards the front' and so forth) and also they will have to describe the surroundings to their followers ('there is a chair on your right, we are going to go between two rows of chairs ...'), so they can create a mental picture of the place and anticipate the moves. When time is up, tell them to switch roles.

2. As a follow-up activity, you can invite the pairs to sit down together and discuss the experience, using the following focus questions or any others you feel would be appropriate for your students:
   □ How did I feel leading and following?
   □ Which was easier for me?
   □ What are some of the qualities of a good leader?

3. With the whole class, ask them to share some of what they discussed.

Note
If you have the opportunity to do Step 1 of this activity in a larger room or outside the building altogether, so much the better.

3.9 The confidence corridor

Focus: This popular self-esteem exercise, which works with the lexical area of positive comments, is aimed at helping learners express words of encouragement to their classmates. It is fun for learners of all ages and for the teacher too, and it is a particularly effective way of creating a feeling of belonging in a group, and making use of authentic affirmative phrases. This activity is most productive when it involves both words and touch, the latter being important to strengthen learners' feeling of acceptance and worth. Perhaps most importantly, the activity creates a positive attitude which can lead to positive outcomes in the classroom.

Level: Elementary +

Time: Lesson 1, 10 minutes; Lesson 2, 20-30 minutes

Preparation: For Lesson 2, bring a CD player to play Track 6 on the CD or some music that gives you a calm and strong feeling.

in class

Lesson 1
1. Lead a brainstorming session to elicit and discuss encouraging words (or phrases and sentences). You can begin by asking your students *What words or phrases would make you feel good or confident?* The answers will vary according to the age and level of the group. Write these on the board.
With beginners, you can ask them to think of very short sentences in their mother tongue, and translate a simple form of these into English.

After class
Write the students' contributions in English on a poster that can be displayed in class, adding any others you think of – see example below. This will serve as a language bank that can grow over a number of lessons as you accumulate contributions.

Lesson 2
2. Draw the students' attention to your poster and get them to read aloud the expressions on it. Deal with any difficulties with pronunciation or meaning.

3. Ask students to form two rows facing each other, making a corridor.

4. Play the music. Ask a student to volunteer to go through the Confidence Corridor that has just been formed. As the student moves slowly between the lines, the others say something encouraging and, if this is acceptable in your classroom situation, touch or pat him or her on the back. Welcome each student at the end of the line, and you too say something special – and genuine! – to that student. The activity is completed when everyone (including you) has gone through the Confidence Corridor.

3.9 The confidence corridor

Variation
As an optional follow-up activity, students pair up and discuss how they felt while walking between the lines. Then ask pairs to share their thoughts with the group. You can ask some of them to tell what they learned from their partner. All this can be done in English or in the mother tongue, according to level.

THE CONFIDENCE CORRIDOR

You can do it. Be confident. Believe in yourself.
You are unique.
Believe in your dreams. Have a wonderful day.
I wish you the best.
Ask for help if you need it. Just do it!
You are part of our group
Your presence makes a difference.
You can make the right choices.
You can be happy. You can learn new things.
You'll be successful.
You can speak in English!

Note
We have found it very useful to do The Confidence Corridor before activities such as group or individual presentations which provide a real challenge for students, when they can benefit from some encouragement from their classmates.

3.10 Hot potato

Focus: To encourage active participation by students. This activity is very good for having fun in the classroom in an orderly way and for creating a relaxed–alert atmosphere where students get involved in speaking, and where they learn to listen to each other and to take turns. It is also an effective way to review vocabulary

Level: Elementary +

Time: 5–10 minutes

Preparation: Bring a CD player and some cheerful, energising music, and a small ball.

in class

1. You can initiate a discussion, ask questions about preferences (favourite colour, favourite part of the day, hobbies and interests), request a personal point of view on a certain subject, or, at the end of class, ask students about what they have learned during the lesson that they want to take with them.

2. Pass a small ball to a student who will answer your question; then this student continues passing the ball to another student who will give his or her answer to your question. It's good to play music while doing this activity, and it's important to keep the ball moving quite quickly, so the body is in the alert state that is generated when playing a game.

3. This can be an indoor activity or an outdoor one.

3.11 Statues

Focus: Speaking. An important purpose of this activity is for students to enjoy a feeling of togetherness and achievement. We generally use this activity at the end of a unit, or when a project has been completed, as a way of celebrating the spirit of learning. It is also used to encourage cooperation and creativity.

Level: Lower intermediate +

Time: 50 minutes

Preparation: Bring in any props that might be useful, and paper and markers for making the posters.

in class

1. Put your students in groups of 5 to 8; tell them that they are going to decide on a scene related to some aspect of life where there would be several people gathered together (football players during a match, a classroom, a family having dinner ...), or they could reproduce a famous work of art or a scene from a well-known film. They should plan this quietly, so the other groups don't hear what they have chosen. Then they decide how they could present the scene, with each of them placed as if they were a statue forming part of the scene. If you feel the choice would be too wide, thus making the guessing over-challenging, you could specify a single theme, e.g. films, or famous pictures.

2. When they are ready, give each group a minute or two to create their scene in front of the class, and then the other groups try to guess what their scene is. If possible, take a digital photo of each scene.

3. After all the groups have presented the scenes they have created together, the students can sit with their group in a circle and discuss the topic of Cooperation. They decide on a group definition and then share with the rest of the class.

4. Finally, in their groups they create posters using words and drawings about Cooperation. Display these in the classroom if possible.

Extension
If in the following class you have access to an interactive whiteboard, you could show photos of the scenes your students created, each on a different page. As you show each photo, give students time to write a sentence about it. Then, project them again, and for each one get a few students to write their sentence on the whiteboard under the photo.

3.11 Statues

Variation
You could project the photos from your computer for students to write down their sentences on a piece of paper, and then when you project a second time, call on several to read their sentences. It can be very enjoyable for them to see their photos and to remember the work they did together.

3.12 Body shop

Focus: This activity can be used as a listening and speaking exercise. It can be a good way to take a kinaesthetic break.

Level: Lower intermediate +

Time: 20 minutes

Preparation: Depending on the level of your class, you may find it necessary to pre-teach the key vocabulary and commands that will be used, and you may want to leave these on the board. Optional: bring in a sheet of sandpaper.

in class

1. Ask for one volunteer to come up the front of the classroom and to stand facing the class, with his or her back to you. Begin by explaining that for the activity one student will be playing the role of the owner of the car, and the other one will be the car itself. Then say the commands given in Step 3 below, and act them out with the volunteer.

2. After this demonstration, keep your volunteer, and the other students find a partner to repeat the procedure. As they are asked to imitate you, this should be easy and fun, because you will be demonstrating the commands again at the front. Repeat the commands, each followed by the appropriate action, until all students respond confidently.

3. Finally, you only say the commands and students act them out completely on their own. When they have done this several times, ask the students to volunteer to take turns in your place, as leader of the activity.
   Commands to be used are the following:
   Take your 'car' out of the garage. (The owner of the car stands behind the car, with his or her hands on their partner's shoulders. Tell them that as the engine is off and lights are out, the car-partners will have their eyes closed. The owner then moves the car gently, two or three steps.)
   Hose your car with water. Splash it all over. (The owner pretends to be using a hose to wash the car.)
   Remove the bumps. (Put one hand on your partner's back, and hold an imaginary hammer with the other one. Hammer gently to remove the bumps on your partner's back.)
   Rub down your car with sandpaper. (You may want to show your students a real piece of sandpaper. The owner firmly rubs their partner's back – **not** using the real sandpaper, though!)
   Ask your car 'What is your favourite colour?' (The car is expected to give an answer. This is the only time when the car is allowed to speak!)

3.12 Body shop

Tell your car 'Imagine that I am painting you in your favourite colour.' Apply several coats of paint. (The owner will pretend to apply several coats of paint with a paint-brush.)
Stand still and admire your car! (Allow several seconds of complete silence, no talking – just feeling.)
Take the car back to the garage.
Switch places!

4. After both students have been the car, the students each find a different partner – maybe someone they have never worked with before – and repeat the activity.

Extension
In groups of 4, the students make posters with the commands taught, using both words and pictures.
An interesting point for discussion could be to allow them to have a few minutes to talk about what they felt during the moment of silence. This can also be used as a springboard for a writing activity.

Note
Confidence is not just related to mental activity; it can also be 'embodied'. Getting in touch through physical contact with others in a safe way such as this can lead to greater confidence overall.

Acknowledgement
We learned this activity from a group of teachers in Sweden.

3.13 The leaders dance

Focus: Speaking. This activity helps to foster a sense of shared leadership in the class. The message is that we can all be leaders.

Level: Lower intermediate +

Time: 30-40 minutes

Preparation: Bring a ribbon for every student, including one gold ribbon; also a CD player to play Track 7 on the CD or some dance music with a strong beat.

in class

Track 7

1. Play the music. Put your ribbons on a table, and ask the students to take one each. Then tell them that the student who has the gold ribbon is going to lead a dance, and the others will imitate his or her movements. After a few moments, he or she will change ribbons with a classmate, who will now be the leader. Continue doing this until several or even all students have had the chance to lead. Ask a few students if they found it easier to lead or to follow.

2. You can then have a class discussion about leadership; this may work better with adults or older secondary students. Use the questions below, or modify them for your students. You may want to work on this using Think-Pair-Share (see p 21).

GOOD LEADERS

1. Make a list of people you feel are good leaders. They may be people you know personally, or they may be well known personalities.
2. Think about these people and write down qualities they share.
3. Are good leaders the same, or are there different ways to be good leaders?
4. Why is a good leader important for a group?

3.14 Signs of the zodiac

Focus: Helping students get to know each other. Speaking and group writing.

Level: Intermediate +

Time: 40–50 minutes

Preparation: Be ready to project the dates for the zodiac signs (dates may vary slightly according to the source). Alternatively, make photocopies, or write/draw it on the blackboard. Make 12 copies of the worksheet (one for each sign).
Optional: for the extension, find a sample horoscope to display or hand out which includes, if possible, points similar to those listed in the extension.

in class

1. Have students get into groups according to their zodiac signs.

* Aries	March 21 – April 20	* Libra	September 24 – October 23
* Taurus	April 21 – May 21	* Scorpio	October 24 – November 22
* Gemini	May 22 – June 21	* Sagittarius	November 23 – December 22
* Cancer	June 22 – July 22	* Capricorn	December 23 – January 20
* Leo	July 23 – August 21	* Aquarius	January 21 – February 19
* Virgo	August 22 – September 23	* Pisces	February 20 – March 20

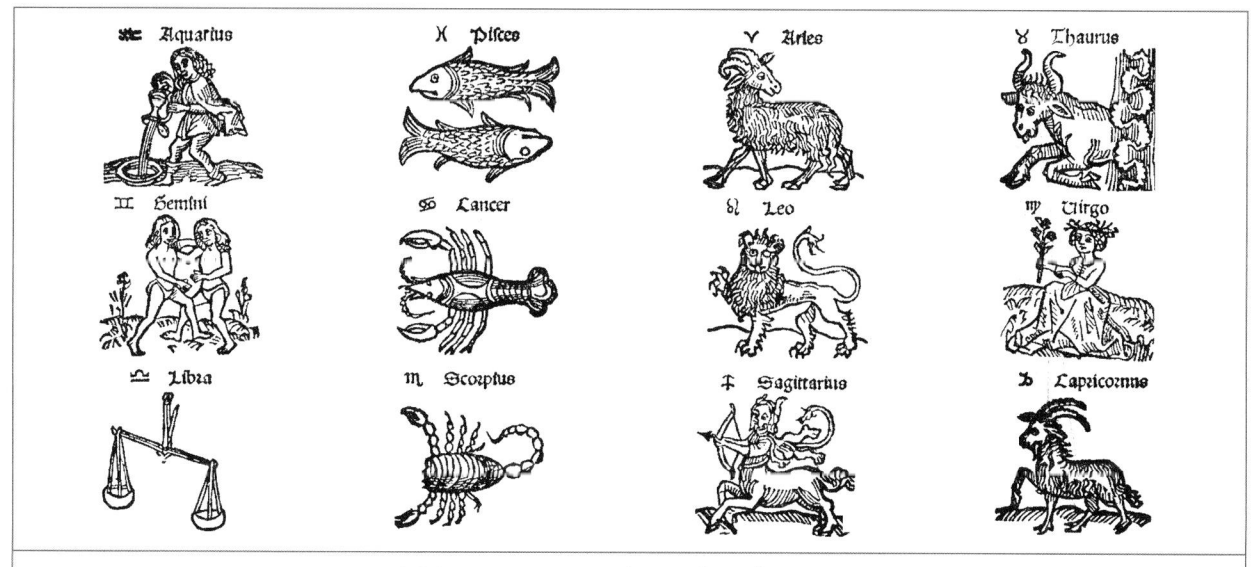

16th century woodcut of Zodiac signs

You may have to make a few changes – for example, if there are a lot of students in one sign you can divide them into two groups. If there are any signs with only one student, they will need to work with one of the other groups.

3.14 Signs of the zodiac

2. Tell the class: *According to some people, when we are born influences how we are. If we assume for the moment that this is true, let's see what you might have in common with the others in your group.*

3. Working in their groups, students find one thing that all agree on for each of the points in the worksheet below; one person can be the secretary and record their answers.

• One thing we like to do at the weekend:
• One place we would all like to visit:
• One thing that bothers us:
• One thing we all look for in a friend:
• One positive quality we all have:
• One goal we have for the future:

4. When they have had time to find their answers, take one point at a time, and each group gives the answer. Call for their answers in a lively way so that this moves quickly.

Extension
In their groups, students write a horoscope description for their sign, based on the information that they have found, and including anything else they would now like to add. You may like to provide them with a sample horoscope to use as a guide. The students should cover at least these aspects:
- ☐ character (your positive traits and your problematic characteristics)
- ☐ what is important for you in life
- ☐ personal relationships with others
- ☐ life projects
- ☐ professions that are good for you.

At this point, collect their compositions, and for the next class you can make photocopies to distribute, or put the compositions up on the walls with blu-tack and have students walk around the class to read what the other groups have written.

3.15 We perform

Focus: Developing a good group atmosphere, which contributes significantly to students' feeling of belonging.

Level: Lower intermediate +

Time: 20-25 minutes

Preparation: Select some sayings with a positive message, one for each four or five students (see **Inspiring Quotations**, Activity 4.4, for some suggestions) and print each saying on different coloured paper. Then cut each saying into several pieces, so you end up with one piece for each of your students; for example, if you have 25 students, cut up 5 sayings into 5 pieces.

in class

1. Mix up your sayings pieces and hand them out in a random manner, one to each student, as they come into the room for their lesson.

2. Students form a group with others who have the same coloured paper. (To make this easier, you might stick up a piece of each colour on the wall in different parts of the room, and they meet by their colour.) They put together their pieces of paper to see what their saying is.

3. You can then tell them something like this: *You all have wonderful sayings that you want to communicate to the rest of the class, so decide how you want to present your saying to them. Maybe you want to sing it, or make a rap, or each person in the group will repeat it in a different way. Maybe you want to mime it or act it out. Be creative!!*

4. After they have had time to decide on their presentation and to rehearse it, call on each group to present their saying. Encourage the class to clap after each presentation.

Note

Group processes are a fundamental factor in the classroom, and can contribute significantly to successful language learning. Dörnyei and Murphey (2003:50) point out that classroom groups go through stages of development: group formation, transition, performing, and dissolution.

Sometimes the performing stage is not emphasised in the classroom – and yet it can be one of the best ways to create a positive group climate; in this activity, we are always surprised at the interest and enthusiasm it generates.

3.16 Today's menu

Focus: Language related to cooking and to emotions

Level: Lower intermediate +

Time: 40–50 minutes

Preparation: Today's Menu (below) to be shown. If you plan to show the menu on a blackboard or poster, consider writing this up before the lesson starts. Photocopies of the three charts below, one set per group of students.

in class

1. Pull Today's Menu up on a page of an interactive whiteboard, project it from your computer or show it on a poster or the blackboard.

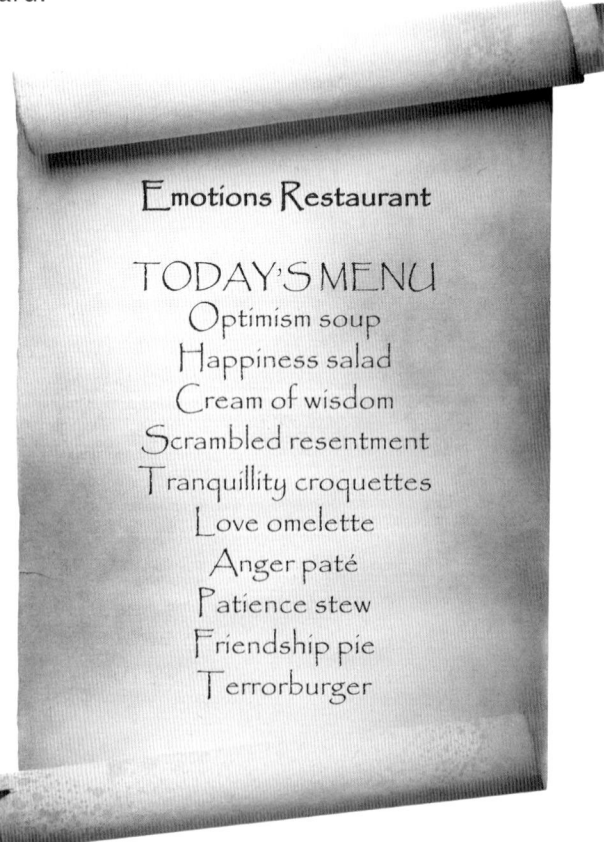

Emotions Restaurant

TODAY'S MENU
Optimism soup
Happiness salad
Cream of wisdom
Scrambled resentment
Tranquillity croquettes
Love omelette
Anger paté
Patience stew
Friendship pie
Terrorburger

2. Explain to students that in small groups they are going to pick a dish to prepare a recipe for.
Once they have decided on their dish, give each group a photocopy of the three charts below. For lower levels you can spend some time clarifying vocabulary that is not clear, or have dictionaries in the room for students to use when they need help. Tell students to work quietly so the other groups don't hear which dish they have chosen.

CHAPTER 3: A SENSE OF BELONGING

3.16 Today's menu

pinch	pound (lb.)
teaspoon (tsp)	ounce (oz.)
tablespoon (tbsp)	slice
drop	can
handful	packet
cup (c.)	pint

add	boil
mix	cook
stir	bake
chop	fry
beat	sauté
drain	cool
cut	freeze
toss	melt
grate	heat
remove	serve (warm, cold ...)
cover	season

joy	cooperation
tenderness	understanding
caresses	generosity
benevolence	energy
nervousness	gratitude
constancy	envy
confidence	stress
irritation	loyalty
calm	determination
peace	ignorance
kisses	satisfaction
fear	tension
good humour	bitterness
bad humour	perseverance
pleasure	empathy
rage	serenity
apprehension	trust
harmony	intuition
hugs	consideration
sincerity	annoyance

3.16 Today's menu

So that your students have an idea about how to write their recipes, you might show them this short example:

> **KINDNESS PUDDING**
> In a bowl, mix 2 cups of empathy and 1 cup of consideration.
> Chop 2 slices of benevolence and add to the first mixture.
> Melt 3 tablespoons of generosity and stir in.
> Still stirring, cook gently over a low heat for 10 minutes.
> Let cool slightly. Serve warm.
> It is also good reheated the next day.

3. When all students have their recipes ready, put up Today's Menu again, and someone from each group will read their recipe to the class, not mentioning the name of their dish. (Alternatively, each group could write the recipe on a transparency for the overhead projector.) The class will try to guess which dish the recipe is for.

4. You can mention that in life you recommend they try the positive 'dishes' and avoid the negative ones.

Extension
As a follow-up, you could have students work in their groups to suggest names for other dishes ('Bravery Appetisers …').

Note
This activity reinforces the feeling of belonging, as the groups have a lot of fun working together writing their recipes, and when they present their work to the rest of the class they get a sense of shared satisfaction from a job well done.

Acknowledgement
A version of this activity was presented by a group of Masters students at the Universidad International Menéndez Pelayo in Santander, Spain.

CHAPTER 4
A SENSE OF PURPOSE

People with goals are successful
because they know what they want
and know where they are going.

Earl Nightingale

Chapter 4: A Sense of Purpose

A sense of purpose is having a feeling of direction and motivation in life. A sense of purpose enables us to enrich our life by setting realistic and achievable goals, taking the necessary actions to accomplish our aims and taking responsibility for our decisions. Without a sense of purpose or direction, we may derive our self-esteem only from others.

Students need to develop a sense of purpose, because this will make their efforts worthwhile. But if their efforts are directed only towards pleasing the demands of others, they will lack internal motivation, which is the greatest source of growth and well-being.

It is especially useful for adolescents to work on building a sense of purpose. When the needs for security, identity and belonging have been satisfied, they can use higher-order thinking processes to set goals and to reflect on the values they hold.

When working on our self-esteem, we can notice the gap between where we are and where we want to be, and then move towards bridging that gap by setting goals and working towards them. Goals give us clear direction for actions which can lead to satisfaction.

As teachers, we may prepare our classes very well, but we always need to keep in mind that teaching is not equal to learning. Students don't always participate actively in their own learning. If we encourage them to set goals and keep their eyes on their goals, this is one way to bring about more active participation.

> **The Sense of Purpose**
> can give meaning to our efforts.
>
> **Teachers who promote a sense of purpose:**
> - transmit positive expectations.
> - show confidence and faith in the abilities of their students.
> - strengthen students' values.
> - help them to set realistic and reachable objectives.

Suggestions for Building a Sense of Purpose

- [ ] Stress to your students the relevance of the things you are teaching them to their personal lives and interests.

- [ ] Ask students to make a list of people they most respect or would like to model their lives after, and then a list of the characteristics they perceive in those people.

- [ ] Share with your students articles about the future – including new developments, inventions, products and social changes taking place around the world – that might affect them at some point.

- Discuss with students the positive traits of movie or TV characters and the values they would probably live by. Get students to compare and contrast their own values with those they perceive in these movie or TV characters.

- Have students identify the values that are most important to them and the code of ethics they are trying to live by. As part of a writing assignment, they can develop a Code of Ethics form; they might take this home to share with others, or hang it in their rooms to serve as a constant reminder of the importance of living by the values they believe in.

- Post sayings or quotations in the classroom that might encourage students to lead inspired lives. Change the sayings every week; students can use the statements as a basis for writing assignments where they explain what the sayings mean to them.

- At the beginning of the year, the students, individually, set a major goal they hope to accomplish by the end of the school year. If possible, post the goals up in the classroom so students will be continually reminded of what they want to accomplish for the year. Switch the goal-notes around from time to time, to help them be seen afresh.

- Encourage students to set goals for the week or the term, that relate to achievement, skill development, personal attitudes and social behaviour, to help them focus on areas in which they want to improve.

- Suggest students make a list at the beginning of each week of the things they want to accomplish during that week. Then they cross the items off as they achieve them. Have them review their list at the end of the week, and determine how they might make the following week more successful.

- Reinforce with students the concept that they can achieve great things if they work toward their goals by taking one small step at a time.

A sense of purpose helps to enable you to:
- become the person you want to be
- achieve your goals,
- solve problems successfully.

A sense of purpose makes effort worthwhile.

4.1 Backward buildup

Focus: Setting language learning goals. Writing.

Level: Lower intermediate +

Time: 25–40 minutes

Preparation: Make a copy of the worksheet for each student, or write it on the board for them to copy.

in class

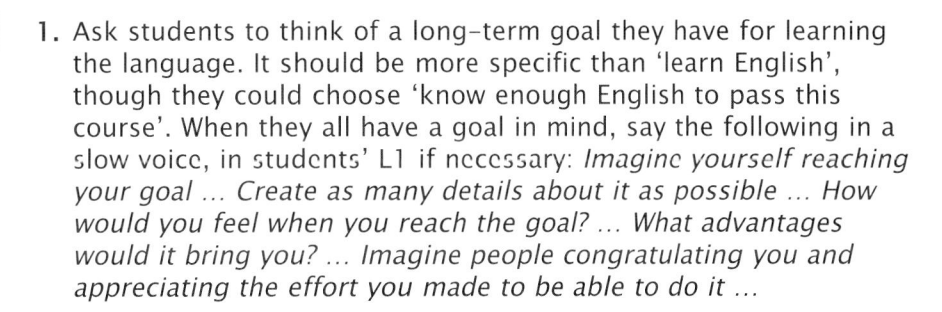

1. Ask students to think of a long-term goal they have for learning the language. It should be more specific than 'learn English', though they could choose 'know enough English to pass this course'. When they all have a goal in mind, say the following in a slow voice, in students' L1 if necessary: *Imagine yourself reaching your goal ... Create as many details about it as possible ... How would you feel when you reach the goal? ... What advantages would it bring you? ... Imagine people congratulating you and appreciating the effort you made to be able to do it ...*

2. Give them a copy of the worksheet. Go over the questions with them, and explain that to get to our goals it is often more useful to start with the goal and work backwards than to start from where we are now.

My goal:

1. How will I feel when I achieve my goal?

2. What are the last steps I will take to reach my goal?

3. How will I feel when I have started to work towards my goal but it is still a bit far away?

4. What are the first steps I will take towards the goal?

5. What will motivate me at the beginning to make the effort to reach my goal?

4.1 Backward buildup

3. As they work individually, circulate to help with any language needed. Give them 10–15 minutes to answer the questions, and then a few minutes to share with the person next to them what their goal was and anything else they would like to say about reaching the goal.

4. As a follow-up, they could write a paragraph to hand in, on the topic 'My goal in language learning and how I am going to reach it', starting from where they are at now, and moving forward.

Note
Backward buildup is a technique that is used with drills in language teaching; it was common in the Audiolingual method. To help students repeat a long sentence in the foreign language, the teacher gives the whole sentence, and then says the end of the sentence for students to repeat, then the part before the end plus the end, and finally the whole sentence. The idea is that this will make it easier to complete the sentence. In a similar way, when students are working with a goal if they see the goal and start from where they are – perhaps a long way from the goal – the way to reach it may not be clear. However, if they get their goal in mind and then imagine having reached it, then imagine the steps taken as they are getting close to reaching it, they can then work their way back to the starting point, and in this way the whole process might seem easier.

Acknowledgement
Sonia López in Murcia, Spain, told us about this technique being used with life goals, and suggested it could be adapted to language goals as well.

4.2 Help yourself

Focus: Language of encouragement. You could do this after **Backward buildup** (Activity 4.1)

Level: Lower intermediate +

Time: 15 minutes

Preparation: A copy of the worksheet for each student.

in class

1. Remind students that there are others who give us a lot of encouragement to reach our goals, but we can also encourage ourselves. Tell them that the images that we see in our minds and the words that we say to ourselves have a lot of power.

2. Have them think of a non-language learning goal they have. Give them a couple of minutes, and then check to be sure everyone has a goal in mind. Then say to them slowly, pausing between each sentence: *See yourself having achieved this goal ... Imagine what it would be like ... What would you do? ... How would you feel?*

3. After giving them a moment to see themselves, remind them that words can help us keep on track. Give them the worksheet, and ask them to complete the sentence 'I see myself ...' with their goal, and then to write 8–10 encouraging statements to themselves.

4. As they work, help them with any language they need. You might ask them to write a draft for you to check first, and then, when it has been corrected, copy the corrected version onto the worksheet. Tell them if they keep this and look at it often, it can help them reach their goal.

4.2 Help yourself

I see myself _____
•
•
•
•
•
•
•
•
•
•

4.2 Help yourself

As a writing model, you could show them the following:

> I see myself practising tai-chi (getting exercise, going jogging ...) 5-10 minutes a day.
> - My body will thank me.
> - I deserve it.
> - I'm making progress.
> - 10 minutes a day is easy to find.
> - Keep going!
> - This is fun!
> - Every day I'm getting better.
> - I can do it!
> - I feel great!
> - Good work! Keep it up!

Variation
After doing the activity with a life goal, you can repeat it another day with a language-learning goal (read a newspaper in English on the internet for five minutes a day, learn ten new phrasal verbs a week ...).

4.3 Words of affirmation

Focus: To help your students to take action toward their goals

Level: Lower intermediate +

Time: 20-25 minutes

Preparation: Some cards or post-it notes.

in class

1. Begin by explaining that an affirmation is a statement of a personal goal, but formulated in such a way as to say that you already have reached that goal or are in the process of doing so. It works best if it comes with a picture in your mind and a feeling. You can mention how top performers in sports regularly use positive affirmations before a race, to get into a supportive state of mind that makes best use of their resources.
   In order to create affirmations that will be most effective, eight rules need to be followed:

   1) Begin with the words 'I AM'. *I am becoming a better learner.*

   2) Affirmations focus on the positive, on what we want; so never use NOT. For example, when taking an exam, a student would not affirm *I am not afraid of exams* but rather *I am calmly answering all the questions in the exam.*

   3) Use the present tense, as if it is happening now: *I am enjoying seeing how much I am learning.*

   4) Keep it short and simple: *I am becoming more and more confident.*

   5) Be specific: *I am happy that I am able to read newspapers in another language.*

   6) Use verbs in the present simple or present continuous: *I am learning more and more each day.*

   7) When appropriate, use a feeling word (adverb): *I am happily working on increasing my vocabulary in my new language.*

   8) Affirmations are about yourself and your own behaviour, not about anyone else.

2. When you have finished this explanation, tell your students to write three affirmations related to their goals on cards or post-it notes. These can include personal goals as well as language learning goals.

4.3 Words of affirmation

3. Then they do an 'affirmation milling' exercise, which consists of moving around the classroom and reading their affirmations to each other.

4. Invite students to say their affirmations to themselves often. They may be surprised at what happens!

Variation
You can ask students to write two copies of their affirmations. One copy they can keep to remind them what their affirmations were and to repeat them to themselves often. The other they hand in; tell them that these will be displayed in the classroom for all students to read, and agree with them whether or not their names are to be shown on these copies.

4.4 Inspiring quotations

Focus: Quotations can provide input for learning the target language; inspirational quotations can help to develop moral values and strengthen our sense of purpose, as well as being a base for working on different language skills. Several ideas for using quotations in the classroom at different moments are given below.

Level: Lower intermediate +

Time: Variable

Preparation: See the different suggestions.

in class

➢ Use quotations to put students into pairs. Print up several quotations, one for every two students (see Quotations Chart at end of Activity). Cut these in half as shown, and give each student one half, then have them walk around trying to find the other part of their quotation to see who their partner for the activity will be.

➢ Regularly – perhaps once a week – begin your class with a new inspirational quotation, e.g. 'In all things we learn only from those we love' (Goethe). Put it up in a prominent place, and ask students to take a few minutes to discuss its meaning with a partner. Then offer some time for sharing their thoughts aloud. Students can be invited to bring their own inspiring quotations; it is very confidence-building for them to see things that they bring in being used for class activities.

➢ Individually or in small groups, students find a quotation in the target language, and prepare a poster using that quotation to be put up on the walls; students then choose the quotation (other than their own) that they like best.
(You should be able to find a collection of quotations at http://www.quoteland.com and at http://en.wikiquote.org/wiki/Main_Page.)

➢ Put a quotation up on the blackboard, and ask students to read it silently for a minute or two. Then quickly erase a few single words here and there. For each blank, ask them to shout out which word they think was erased.

➢ Every Monday, write an inspiring quotation on the board. Your students can copy these in the understanding that when the next exam comes they will get extra credit for the quotations they remember. This suggestion comes from María Santos, an EFL teacher in Murcia, Spain, who comments that if she forgets to write the Quotation for the Week on the board, her students will

4.4 Inspiring quotations

remind her to put it up – and even teachers in other subject areas ask her for the quotations or translations of them in Spanish.

➢ Put up posters with quotations round the classroom. You can easily make these by finding quotations you like and printing them out on coloured paper. Play some music, and give students a few moments to walk around the classroom and read them all. Stop the music, and tell them to stand by the one they like best and, with others who also chose it, discuss questions such as the following: Why did you choose it? What does it say to you? In what way do you feel identified with the quotation? As they are discussing the questions you can walk around and check what they have to say, or after the discussion time you can have each group summarize in a sentence or two their ideas for the whole class.

➢ With students in groups of 4, hand out a list of five or more quotations with gaps. In their groups, students try to fill in the gaps with appropriate words. Elicit from different groups their suggestions for completion before giving them the original versions. Sometimes students' versions are an improvement on the original quotation!

4.4 Inspiring quotations

QUOTATIONS CHART	
If you think you can	or think you can't … you are right. (Henry Ford)
In all things we only learn	from those we love. (Goethe)
You make the world a better place	by making yourself a better person. (Scott Sorrell)
The first step to wisdom is silence	the second is listening. (Ibn Gabirol)
Problems are what you see	when you take your eyes off your goal. (Hannah More)
Who looks outside dreams,	who looks inside awakens. (Carl Jung)
We don't know who we are until we can	see what we can do. (Martha Grimes)
Everything you can imagine	is real. (Picasso)
We must learn to live together as brothers or	perish together as fools. (Martin Luther King)
If you are not happy	here and now, you will never be happy. (Taisen Deshimaru)
You've got to jump off cliffs all the time	and build your wings on the way down. (Ray Bradbury)
We either make ourselves miserable or make	ourselves strong. The amount of work is the same. (Carlos Castaneda)
Following another's path leads to	who they are, not who you are. (Harry Palmer)
Some see things as they are and say 'Why?'	I dream things that never were and say 'Why not?' (George Bernard Shaw)
We become what we think	about all day long. (Ralph Waldo Emerson)
Be the change you	want to see in the world. (Gandhi)
Try first to understand, then	to be understood. (Stephen Covey)
Luck is what happens when preparation	meets opportunity. (Seneca)
Kindness is a language that the deaf	can hear and the blind can see. (Mark Twain)

4.5 Eyes on the goal

Focus: Speaking and listening. To allow your students to take responsibility for their outcomes, stay focused on what they want to achieve, and take the steps necessary to get there. This activity may be best for older secondary and adult students.

Level: Lower intermediate +

Time: 30 minutes

Preparation: A worksheet for each student.

in class

1. Ask your students to think about their lives, and bring to mind an important goal that they have and write it down in one sentence. It should be a goal they are comfortable sharing with others.

2. Then put them into pairs and give each student a worksheet. They are going to take turns to ask and answer a set of seven questions that can help them learn to keep their eyes upon their goals. Ask them to decide who will be A and who will be B. A will ask the questions and will write down the main ideas of what B answers. At this point A asks only the questions on the worksheet. Then they switch roles.

3. When they have both answered the questions, they can discuss the activity, asking each other about anything they found interesting.

4. Then they give each other the notes they have taken, and they each write up a paragraph about their goal based on the notes, adding anything else they would like to say. Collect the paragraphs and correct them, adding any comments or suggestions about reaching their goals. Give them back the next day, and the students copy the corrected version to keep in their notebook to read when they want.

Extension
At the end of a month or towards the end of the course, for homework you could have them go back to what they wrote and write a paragraph on any progress made towards their goal.

4.5 Eyes on the goal

Seven questions to help you keep your eyes on your goal:
1. What do you really want to achieve?
2. Why do you want it?
3. What are you doing to get there?
4. Is what you are doing/thinking/ helping you?
5. Is there anything you could change to move forward more effectively? (Beliefs, actions, self-talk …)
6. What is your major challenge?
7. What extra help might you need? (resources, strategies, etc)

Note
If appropriate, they can use goals related to their studies or to learning the language; however, we have found that using other types first may be more useful for them to see the effects of working on goals. You might suggest they think of goals such as using their time better or being calmer.

4.6 Formula for success

Focus: Reading and speaking. Using images to achieve goals.

Level: Intermediate +

Time: Lesson 1, 25 minutes; Lesson 2, 20-30 minutes.

Preparation: Print a copy of the story for each four students, and cut it into four pieces. Have the slide (at the end of the activity) ready to show on an interactive whiteboard or project on the computer. Alternatively, write its words on a poster or on the blackboard, and cover them till you are ready to show them.

in class

Lesson 1

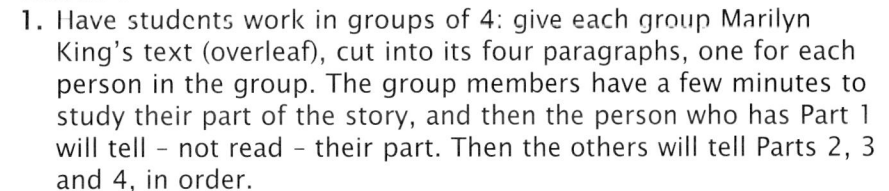

1. Have students work in groups of 4: give each group Marilyn King's text (overleaf), cut into its four paragraphs, one for each person in the group. The group members have a few minutes to study their part of the story, and then the person who has Part 1 will tell – not read – their part. Then the others will tell Parts 2, 3 and 4, in order.

2. Write on the board FORMULA FOR SUCCESS, and ask your students to write down what they think her formula was. Accept any answers, and then show the slide on an interactive whiteboard, project it from your computer or show it on a poster or the blackboard.

3. Tell students that if we have an image which represents our goal, when we see that image it will remind us of the goal, and so remind us that we need to keep working towards it.

Lesson 2

Before class: the students think of a goal they have – not necessarily related to language learning – and an image to associate with it. They could find something on the internet and send it to you by email to show in class on an interactive whiteboard, or they could make a drawing or find a photo and make a little poster.
In class: students can take turns to show the image they have selected, and their classmates try to guess their goal. If they don't guess quickly, the student can reveal what the goal is and why the image represents their goal.

4.6 Formula for success

1. As a teenager in the US, Olympian Marilyn King was an average student who enjoyed sports. When her school needed a participant for a pentathlon competition – one with five different events – she volunteered, and she came in third! Then she trained a little, and the next year came in first; and then she went to a national competition and was in the top ten. The Olympic committee was there, and they chose two girls that she had beaten, even though she knew she was definitely better than one. At first, she was disappointed, but then she realised something: 'If they chose her and I beat her, that means **I could go to the Olympics!**'

2. She started imagining walking one day into the Olympic stadium on opening day, and suddenly her training became easier and she was more motivated. Marilyn was not really much different from other teenagers, When the alarm clock rang at five in the morning for her workout, she had a tendency to think, 'I'm too tired' – but as she lay in bed, the image of herself walking into the Olympic stadium would come into her head, and she would smile and get excited. And she would get up and run!

3. Marilyn realised her dream, and competed in two Olympics. She decided to try once more, and devoted a whole year to training. Then nine months before the national trials for the Olympics she had a terrible car accident. For four months she was in great pain and had to lie on her couch without moving, but she started watching videos of the best people in each of her five events, and this distracted her from her pain. She started imagining it was her and practising mentally. She kept sending little messages to her muscles telling them what to do. Finally, before the trials, she could move – and with very little preparation, she came in second!

4. Later in her life, she talked with many groups of ex-Olympians to study what it was that made them successful. She discovered that most had a clear vision of what they wanted, and this vision was strongly present in their minds. Their vision, or goal, also inspired great passion and excitement in them; the vision and the passion inspired them to take a lot of action. In her own life, she found that once the vision got big and the passion grew, the actions she needed to take just suddenly appeared. But without the image, the 'how-to-do it' doesn't come.

Acknowledgement
This is adapted from the story of Marilyn King in Tim Murphey's *Language Hungry!*, 2006 (Helbling Languages).

4.6 Formula for success

Variation
For Step 1, instead of dividing up the reading, you can have students look at the following sentences and decide if they think that they are true or false. Then they read the whole story to check, correcting any that are false.

1. The Olympic athlete, Marilyn King, had always been very good at sports.
2. Since she was a child, she had the idea of going to the Olympics.
3. In her second year of training, she was in the top ten in the US national competition.
4. She could train hard because she wasn't like most other teenagers.
5. When she had a bad car accident, she practised by imagining herself competing.
6. She couldn't ever compete again because of her injury.
7. Later she talked to Olympians and found that they were successful because they had superior physical attributes.

Note
If your students are interested, you could tell them that Marilyn King did research into the importance of imagery and mental rehearsal, and learned at the National Institute of Mental Health that the brain actually changes as a result of mental rehearsal. And what she found was really important for peak performance is the union of passion, vision (the image) and action.

From the insights from her research and her extensive conversations with Olympic athletes in 1980, she created a company called Olympian Thinking, and has worked since then with business, education and peace organisations.

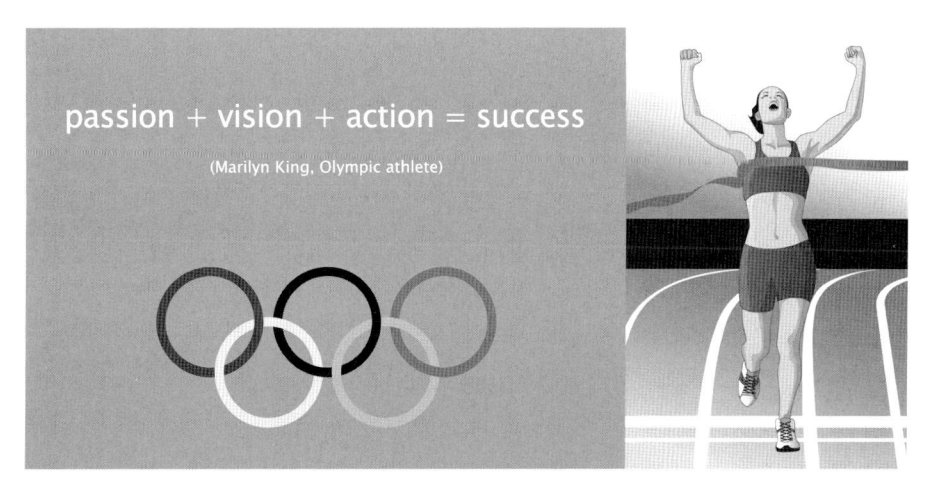

passion + vision + action = success

(Marilyn King, Olympic athlete)

4.7 Great dreams

Focus: Listening and writing. To make students aware of the power of our dreams to lead to realisations.

Level: Upper intermediate +

Time: 40–50 minutes

Preparation: Optional: download John Lennon's *Imagine*. You should be able to find it on youtube or a similar site.
Find a basic biography of Martin Luther King; perhaps download it from here:
http://www.bbc.co.uk/history/historic_figures/king_martin_luther.shtml
Make a copy of the biography for each student.
Download a video of Martin Luther King's speech 'I have a dream', and prepare to project it.
(For lower levels, you may be able to find versions with subtitles in students' L1.)
Bring in a CD player to play Track 8 on the CD or some other quiet music. Compose a sentence about something you feel would be important, not just for you but for the world: 'I have a dream that …'

in class

1. Ask your students if they can think of any people throughout history who have had dreams that led them to have a great impact on the world. Your students might mention Columbus, Gandhi, the Wright brothers or others. At this point, you might show them the video of John Lennon's *Imagine*, or play the song on a CD.

2. Hand out your short biography of Dr Martin Luther King, and ask your students to read about him. As they read, they underline any words they don't know. Clear up important doubts, then ask them to read it again and choose one sentence that they particularly like.

3. Go around the room for everyone in turn to read their sentence aloud. Tell them that it doesn't matter if they have chosen the same sentence as others.

4. Explain that they are going to listen to Dr King giving a part of his famous speech, 'I have a dream'. Let them know that they won't be tested on it, so they can just relax and listen.

5. After listening to the speech, they brainstorm any words, ideas and feelings they remember, and write these on the board.

4.7 Great dreams

6. Play the music while the students complete the sentence 'I have a dream that … ' Ask them to think of something they feel would be important, not just for them but for the world. Let them have 3 or 4 minutes.

7. With the students in a circle if possible, tell them your own sentence, then go around the room for each person to read theirs; the others are to listen in silence and make no comments.

4.8 What makes your heart sing?

Focus: Speaking and writing. To give students a sense of purpose by connecting themselves with their dreams, and teach them to transform their dreams into goals.

Level: Lower intermediate +

Time: 30 minutes

Preparation: Photocopy the starter letter, or prepare to project it, or write it on the blackboard. Bring in a CD player to play Track 9 on the CD or some other soft, relaxing music and bring in a little ball.

in class

Track 9

1. Begin with a relaxation exercise. You can modify the script according to the age and language level of your students. Play the music and say: *Get into a comfortable position, with your eyes closed, or focused on a spot on the floor ... breathe in and out very gently ... feel the air coming in ... fresh air comes in ... imagine that you are taking the air to every cell of your body ... and then let the air out ... exhale ... imagine that as you exhale, you let go of your worries or anxieties, you let go of thoughts related to things you have to do ... enter a state where you are fully present, fully you ... enter a state of 'being', being here in this moment and place ... and notice how your mind and body are much more receptive and relaxed ...*
Now imagine yourself doing something that would make your heart sing ... *It can be a holiday you want to take, a place you want to visit, a conversation you want to have, someone you want to know, a skill you would like to develop, an instrument you would like to play ... imagine yourself doing what would make your heart sing and feeling happy.*

2. Allow a few moments to pass, and then tell your students: *Start focusing on your breathing again, on the air that goes in and out ... Now open your eyes, gently with no rush, make contact with the classroom, with the physical space, with the people around.* When they have all opened their eyes, invite them to work in pairs, and share their experience with each other. While they are doing this, play the same background music that you used during the relaxation exercise.

3. After about 5 minutes, invite them to share what would make their heart sing with the whole class. To start this, throw the ball to a student (or ask who would like to share), and then when that student has finished, tell them to throw the ball to someone else. You can continue this moment of whole-class sharing for the time you consider appropriate, bearing in mind that it is better to stop while the interest is still high.

4.8 What makes your heart sing?

4. Have your students write a letter to anyone they like about what makes their heart sing. The person they write to can be someone they know, or someone famous. It could even be you!
Collect these, but instead of correcting errors, consider writing a short individual comment of encouragement on each one.

Dear _____ ,

I would like to tell you about a dream I have, something that would make my heart sing.

I would like to …

This is important for me because …

What I could do to begin to make this dream come true is …

Some help I might need would be …

Sincerely,
_____ (name)

Note
You may want to practice the relaxation activity before using it in class.

4.9 Turning dreams into smart goals

Focus: Writing. To give students a sense of purpose by helping them learn to transform their dreams into goals. (This activity works well if done after **What makes your heart sing?** Activity 4.8.)

Level: Lower intermediate +

Time: 25-35 minutes

Preparation: Make photocopies of the Smart Goals worksheet, or write it on the board.

in class

1. Have your students think of dreams they have: things they would really be interested in learning or achieving. You can begin by giving an example yourself, e.g. 'One thing I would like to achieve is to be able to play a musical instrument'. Tell them that they are going to make a list of dreams and then to choose one dream and turn it into a goal. To get them thinking, you can list on the board areas to consider. Choose these according to their age and interests.

For adults, some examples might be:	For adolescents, some examples might be:
☐ Family	☐ Studies
☐ Friends/Relationships	☐ Friends/Relationships
☐ House	☐ Hobbies
☐ Recreation/Sports	☐ Future career
☐ Job/Career/Business	☐ Service
☐ Service/Community/World	

Explain to your students that in order to live a balanced life, we need to set goals for different aspects of our life, but in this activity they are going to work on just one area, and focus on only one goal.

2. Then tell them that in order to transform wishes or dreams into **smart goals**, some specific aspects need to be considered. For a goal to be SMART, it should be:

SMART GOALS
Specific: It should be detailed enough for anyone to understand it
Measurable: What evidence are you going to gather to measure your success?
Achievable: Is this achievable by you? Only YOU can answer this!
Responsible: Is this good for you? Is it good for others?
Time-bound: When is the deadline? (It is said that the difference between a dream and a goal is a deadline!)

4.9 Turning dreams into smart goals

Tell your students that SMART goals are specific and measurable, so they need to ask themselves '**What do I really want**?' This is the most important question to answer. Explain that for achieving our goals it is usually very helpful to write them down. And it is very important to feel the joy and happiness that imagining yourself achieving the goal brings with it!

3. After this explanation, tell your students to choose one dream or one wish from their list, and write a SMART goal following the guidelines specified above. For example, with the goal 'To become a good chess player', for the S (Specific) they might write 'I want to be able to play chess in a tournament'. Help them with any language they need in order to complete the goal. When they have finished, tell them to share what they have written with a partner.

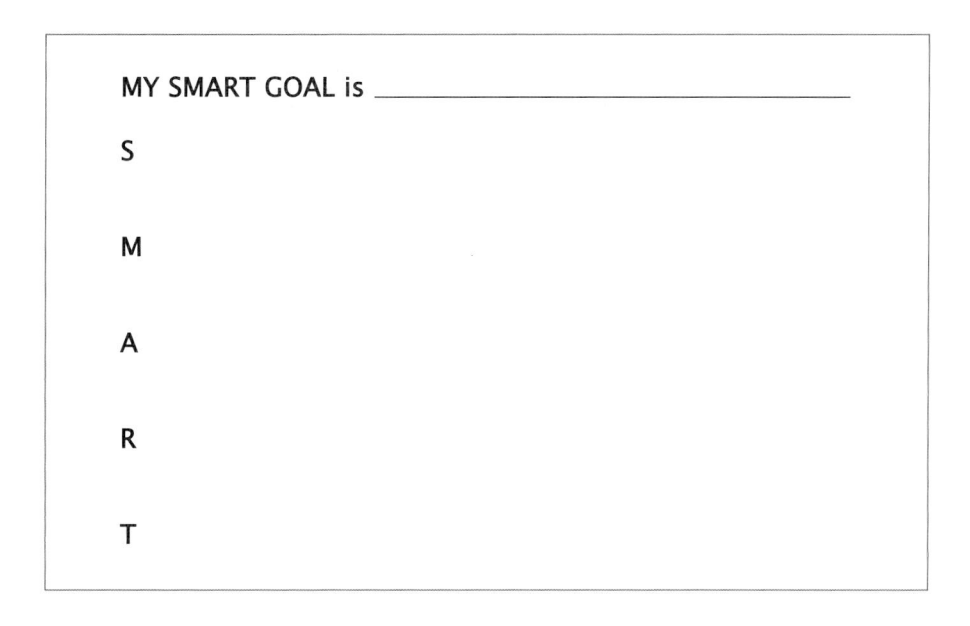

MY SMART GOAL is _____

S

M

A

R

T

---

4. You can end the activity by inviting students who are willing to do so, to share their goals with the whole class.

Extension
Invite your students to write specific objectives for other areas of their life. These don't have to be major goals; small goals are also important. Tell them to choose a few to share with the whole class next time.

4.9 Turning dreams into smart goals

Variation
Begin the activity by writing the following on the board for students to copy, and then they make a wish list of several things they would like to be/have/do.

I WOULD LIKE TO:		
BE:	HAVE:	DO:

4.10 Visualise your goals

Focus: To help your students accomplish their goals. This could be done before or after **Formula for Success**, Activity 4.6.

Level: Intermediate +

Time: 15 minutes

Preparation: Bring a CD player to play Track 10 on the CD or some background music.

in class

1. Begin by explaining that we all have an extraordinary power within us called 'visualisation', which has been used for decades by Olympic athletes and peak performers. When used to improve performance in any skill, it is often called 'mental rehearsal'. Using this power can rapidly accelerate the accomplishment of goals. You could also explain that visualisation:
   * programs the brain to identify resources needed to accomplish the goals.
   * enhances motivation and gives the strength to take the steps to reach those goals.
   * generates creativity by activating the subconscious mind.

   Finally, explain that the procedure of using visualisations is indeed very easy, that all you need is to find a quiet place and time to do it. Tell your students that they are going to experience it now!

2. Play the CD, or play your music while you say the following in a soft voice:

   We are going to create a movie in our minds. To do so, it is easier if you close your eyes or at least look down ... Adjust your body until you find a comfortable position ... Now imagine one of your goals, something you really want to achieve ... It can be about your studies ..., about learning a new skill ..., making new friends ..., your holidays ... think of something that is good and important for you ... something that you really want to achieve ...

   Allow a few moments and then continue with the following steps:

   ☐ *I invite you to make a picture in your mind, about your goal, and imagine yourself doing it, achieving it ... project that image into a screen, imagine it as a movie ... see yourself in detail In this movie, doing what you want to achieve ... add colours, sounds ... see your own face and body movements ... see if there are people around you .... Can you see yourself? What are you doing, saying? ... How are you feeling? Stay there for a moment, connected to this image and your feelings ... become one with the image that is projected of yourself. And now, experience the whole thing again, you are in the movie! What are you doing? How are you feeling? Stay connected to this for a moment ...*

4.10 Visualise your goals

> ☐ *Take a few deep breaths ... and now bring yourself back to this room, to this here and now ... come back, bringing the image of that movie in your mind, and the feelings that you experienced in your heart .... When you find it comfortable for you ... open your eyes again.*

3. Give your students a few minutes to talk about their visualisation in pairs. Make sure everyone has a partner; if necessary you can have a group of 3.

4. When they have completed this part, invite students to talk about the visualisation with the whole class.

5. You can end your class by explaining that if they practise visualisations on a daily basis, they are likely to be pleasantly surprised by the results.

Note
This works best when you have established a comfortable atmosphere within the group.
For lower levels, you could do the visualisation in students' L1, and then have them use their experience as a basis for the discussion with a partner in the L2 in Step 3.

4.11 Seeing your language self

Focus: Writing and speaking. You might like this to follow **Visualise your goals**, Activity 4.10. Here, you are applying the power of visualisation for goal-setting to the language learning context.

Level: Lower intermediate +

Time: 30–40 minutes

Preparation: Make copies of the worksheet / write it on the board.

in class

1. With the Think-Pair-Share technique (see p 21), students work on this topic: 'What are the advantages of speaking the target language?' Depending on their age, you may see advantages ranging from understanding songs or information on the internet to getting job promotion.

2. Say to your students: *Think of some good qualities you have .... Then think of other qualities you would like to have .... Now imagine that you have the ability to speak English very well .... See all the things you can do .... Enjoy how it feels to speak English well ...* Give them time to visualise this.

3. Show the table on the board for students to copy, or hand out the photocopies:

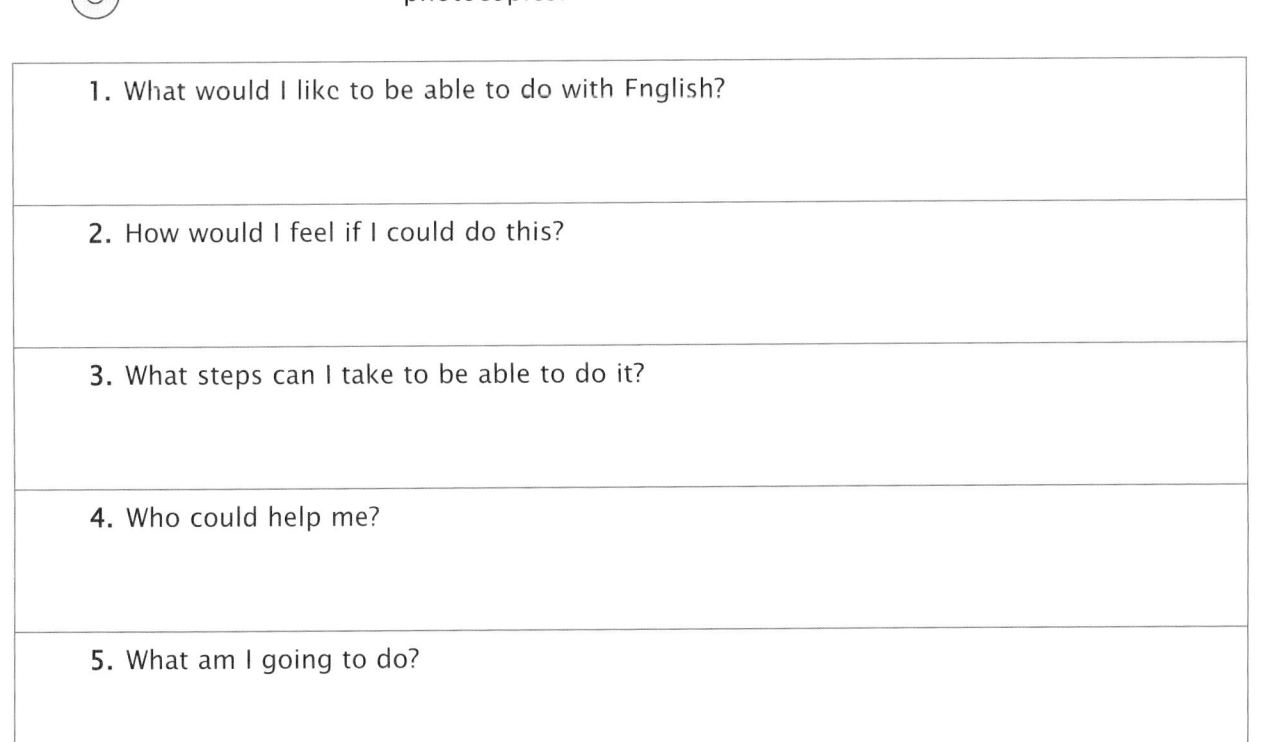

1. What would I like to be able to do with English?
2. How would I feel if I could do this?
3. What steps can I take to be able to do it?
4. Who could help me?
5. What am I going to do?

4.11 Seeing your language self

4. In pairs, the students exchange worksheets, and ask each other any questions they can think of about what their partner has written on his/her worksheet.

5. The pairs find another pair to work with, and each person presents their partner's answers. For example, A would say to C and D, 'B would like to be able to speak English well to talk with more people when she travels. She would feel much more confident if she could do this ...'

Notes

1. Dörnyei (2005) has explained that a very powerful motivational factor is our image of the self we would like to become, our ideal self. This is so, because if we imagine ourself having a quality which is attractive to us, this gives us energy to take the action necessary to achieve that state or that goal. If speaking the foreign language is part of our ideal self, we have a much better chance of successful learning.

2. In his article 'Positive Image, Positive Action: The Affirmative Basis of Organising' (http://www.stipes.com/aichap2.htm), David Cooperrider tells us:
'All of our cognitive capacities—perception, memory, learning—are cued and shaped by the images projected through our expectancies. We see what our imaginative horizon allows us to see. And because 'seeing is believing', our acts often take on a whole new tone and character depending on the strength, vitality, and force of a given image.'

4.12 A world of values

Focus: Speaking. Lexical area of values.

Level: Lower intermediate +

Time: 40–50 minutes

Preparation: Bring a CD player to play Track 9 of the CD or other background music. Optional: prepare a poster with the values words to project from your computer or put up on the wall.

in class

1. Ask students to brainstorm values they feel are important. Write these on the board, translating from their L1 if necessary. After you have a good list, you could add any you would like to complete the list or you could show the chart and explain words that your students might not know.

2. Play the music, and ask the students to look at the list for a few minutes and select the value they feel is most important to them at this moment. Then the students get up and walk around if space permits, saying their value to a few others. After a few moments say *Stop!* or *Freeze!*

3. With others near them, they form groups of 3 or 4 and sit together in a circle. They take turns talking about their value – why they chose it, what it means to them, etc. This can be done as a sentence completion exercise, eg. *I chose patience because* ... (see **Circle Time**, Activity 2.5).

4. After they have all had time in their groups to speak, tell them they are going to create something with the value words chosen by those in their group; it can be a poem, a paragraph, a story, combining the values they have chosen. They decide a way to present it to the rest of the class (a poster, a mini presentation, a dialogue, etc). Walk around, giving the groups any help needed.

5. Each group presents their creation to the rest of the class.

Extension

Leave the chart on the wall another day, and in groups or in pairs students think of a well-known person who exemplifies one of the values. As an outside-class project, they prepare an oral presentation about the person to give in class or a written one to display in the classroom for others to read.

Note

A sense of purpose is related to having realistic and achievable goals. Values can inspire and clarify those goals. Students who set goals inspired in values are likely to be self-motivated and more responsible in the classroom

4.12 A world of values

A WORLD OF VALUES

Generosity	Individuality
Integrity	Simplicity
Justice	Tranquility
Love	Progress
Diversity	Honour
Peace	Strength
Reliability	Truth
Resourcefulness	Tolerance
Confidence	Unity
Responsibility	Wisdom
Stability	Patience
Beauty	Flexibility
Commitment	
Bravery	Happiness
Patience	Trust
Competence	Friendship
Cooperation	Freedom
Tolerance	Wisdom
Creativity	Gratitude
Discipline	Concern for others
Loyalty	Honesty
Respect	Endurance
Equality	Harmony
Good will	Carefulness

4.13 We can choose

Focus: Speaking. This activity is designed to make students more aware that they have choices. While they may not always be able to choose the circumstances, they can choose their attitude, and this can make a great difference. Attitude is a vital factor influencing our ability to reach our goals.

Level: Intermediate +

Time: 20 minutes (or with the Variation, 40–50 minutes)

Preparation: Make copies of the A and B cards.

in class

1. Divide the class into two groups, A and B. Give each group their corresponding card, using Set 1 for adults and Set 2 for secondary students. Don't tell them what is on the other group's card.

2. Give them several minutes to get into their role, to see themselves in the situation described, to think of details about each aspect, and to imagine what they would say to someone about what they are feeling now about everything in their situation.

3. Match up each A with a B. If there is an uneven number of students, be prepared to participate yourself. Tell them to talk to each other about their life now, and to make it very clear how they are feeling about it. They should listen to their partner, but then bring forth their ideas about their own situation, giving arguments about why they feel the way they do.

4. After they finish, they could get into groups with another pair and decide on a sentence that summarizes the main implication of the activity. A good answer would be 'Your attitude determines how you live a situation', but accept all answers. If you are using the Extension, you may prefer to do this step at the end of the story-telling.

Set 1

A

You are a rather pessimistic person, and you are particularly upset now because of several things:
- ☐ You have to move to a new house.
- ☐ Your daughter is going to move in with you.
- ☐ You are going to have a new boss at work.

4.13 We can choose

> **B**
>
> You are a very optimistic person, and you are particularly happy now because of several things:
> ☐ You have to move to a new house.
> ☐ Your daughter is going to move in with you.
> ☐ You are going to have a new boss at work.

Set 2

> **A**
>
> You are usually worried about something, and you are really upset now because of several things:
> ☐ Your friend who lives next door is moving to another city.
> ☐ You are getting a new teacher tomorrow.
> ☐ A party on Saturday evening has been cancelled.

> **B**
>
> You are usually very happy, and you are particularly pleased now because of several things:
> ☐ Your friend who lives next door is moving to another city.
> ☐ You are getting a new teacher tomorrow.
> ☐ A party on Saturday evening has been cancelled.

At the end, you could tell your students the following joke:
There were twin brothers and one was a terrible pessimist – always negative – and the other was an incredible optimist – happy no matter what happened.
Their parents wanted to see if they might change, and so for their birthday they took the pessimist outside and showed him a beautiful pony they had bought for him. He looked at it and grumbled, 'I'd fall off if I tried to ride it. And it would run away. I don't want it!'
Then they told the optimist he could get his present in the garage. When he went in, he saw the garage was full of horse manure. A long time passed and he didn't come out, so the parents went in and there he was happily shovelling the horse manure and saying, 'Where there is this much horse manure there must be a horse.'

Extension
To work on reading and speaking, make one copy of the following story for each group. Cut the text into its four parts, and give one part to each person in the group; they have 5 minutes to study their part of the text. Then the students with Part 1 of the story tell (not

4.13 We can choose

read) their part of the story, in their own words, to the rest of the group. Then the other group members tell their parts in order.

Asclepius and the Two Travellers

1. Asclepius was once walking in the countryside outside Athens. At noon, the sun was high in the sky and he had been walking since dawn. As the sun beat down, he became aware that he was feeling very hot and thirsty. Then nearby he heard the sound of water. He followed the sound and came to a small stream. He sat down thankfully in the cool shade and rinsed his hands in the water. It felt refreshingly cold. He cupped his hands together, filled them with the pure water and raised it to his lips. Nothing had ever tasted so wonderful.

2. Just at that moment, a traveller came by.
   'Excuse me,' said the man, 'I'm going to Athens and I've never been there before. Have you any idea what it's like?'
   'Where have you come from?' asked Asclepius.
   'Piraeus,' said the man.
   'Well, what's that like?' asked Asclepius.
   'Oh it's a dreadful place,' said the man. 'Full of traffic and noise and dirt and unfriendly people. It's a terrible place.'
   'Well, I expect you'll find Athens just the same,' said Asclepius.
   'Oh dear,' said the man, and he walked sadly on his way.

3. Asclepius realised that he was feeling quite hungry after all his walking. Out of his pack he took the food he had brought with him. First there was a nice loaf of bread, freshly baked that morning. He took a deep breath and enjoyed the smell of it for a moment. Then he took out some white, sharp feta cheese made from his own goats' milk, and big black olives. And to follow this, he had brought a large sweet juicy orange. His mouth was watering with anticipation, when he was interrupted by another traveller.

4. 'Excuse me,' said the second man. 'I'm going to Athens and I've never been there before. Have you any idea what it's like?'
   'Where have you come from?' asked Asclepius.
   'Piraeus,' said the second man.
   'Well, what's that like?' asked Asclepius.
   'Oh it's a wonderful place,' said the man. 'Full of life and joy and colour and friendly people. It's a fantastic place.'
   'Well, I expect you'll find Athens just the same,' said Asclepius.
   'Oh good,' said the man, and he walked happily on his way. Asclepius smiled and bit into his bread. It was delicious.

4.13 We can choose

Acknowledgements
The Asclepius story is adapted from J Revell and S Norman's *In Your Hands: NLP in ELT*, 1997 (Saffire Press).
We got the idea for the first part of this activity from J Hadfield and C Hadfield's *Advanced Communication Games*, 1987 (Nelson).

4.14 My mission/ life purpose statement

Focus: To provide your students with the opportunity to connect themselves with their values, talents and ideals. This activity is a very good way to inspire your students to compose a personally meaningful text. You might want to explain first that many companies and organisations have mission statements to define what they stand for and what they aspire to do, what their values and objectives are. The statements are reference points which help those involved to keep in mind where they are going.

Level: Lower intermediate +

Time: 20 minutes

Preparation: None.

in class

1. Tell your students to think of two words that express positive personal qualities that they have: e.g. *imagination* and *enthusiasm*.

2. They write down two verbs related to ways they would like to express those qualities in their everyday life, at home, in the classroom, at work: e.g. *support* and *nurture*.

3. Next, tell them to think of their ideal world. You can do this in the form of a short guided visualisation: *I'd like to invite you now to think of your ideal world ... what would it look like? ... see some of the details of this world ... what kinds of people are there? ... how do they interact? ... what are you doing in this perfect place?* or as a brainstorming session with all the class making suggestions for what an ideal world would be like. Allow a few moments and then tell them each to write down a statement in present tense describing this place, e.g: *It is a place full of love and joy!*

4. Ask them to combine all the words, adding a few more if needed, and create a text, e.g: *My purpose in life is to use my imagination and enthusiasm, to support and nurture others, as we all express our talents in loving and joyful ways!*

5. Give them some time to complete their mission statement. As they will finish at different times, you can tell them that when they are done, to put up their hands so they can see who else has finished, and then they can get into pairs or small groups, to read their texts to each other. If possible, make a place in the classroom where they can put up their Mission Statements.

Acknowledgement
Verónica learned this activity at Jack Canfield's Facilitation Skills Seminar.

4.15 The end

Focus: As language learning is a lifelong process, it is important for students to end a course with a positive feeling about it so that they will be more disposed to continue working later towards their learning goals. For this reason, it is a good idea to provide an adequate closing for the course.

Level: Elementary +

Time: 20 minutes

Preparation: Provide three pieces of coloured paper about 10 cm (4 in) square for each student. Bring in a CD player to play Track 7 on the CD or some other cheerful music.
For Variation 1, write on a piece of coloured paper a positive message from you to each of your students.
For Variation 3, bring in a box of sweets with enough for all your students, plus stiff paper or card, and coloured pens/pencils.
For Variation 4, bring in a supply of special paper, one piece per pair of students.

in class

1. At the end of the last class of the course, put students into groups of 4, and give each student the three pieces of coloured paper.

2. While you play the music, students will write positive messages on the pieces of paper for each of the others in their group. Remind them that we all have a lot of good qualities and that now we want to focus on these. When they have finished, they hand out their messages to the other three students.

Variations

1. To help them get started, you can hand out the messages from you for everyone in the class. If the class is too large for you to write individual notes, you could use something like this for all of them:
   - You have contributed to making this an enjoyable class for me.
   - Remember to dream big.
   - 'The future belongs to those who believe in the beauty of their dreams' (Eleanor Roosevelt).

2. For lower levels you may want to provide structures (*I'm glad you were in my class because ....*) into which they can insert more specific information from vocabulary banks or with your help.

3. Closing can also come into focus at other moments in the course. For example, on the last day of class before a long holiday, you could have the students write their name on a small piece of

4.15 The end

paper and put all the names in a box with sweets in it. Then each student takes a sweet and draws a name. Hand out the paper and coloured pencils or pens for them to make a card with a positive message for the person whose name they have drawn. Play the music while they work. Pick up the cards and hand them out to the person they were written for.

4. If you have planned for students to work on several activities in pairs where you have paired them in a random manner, save 15 minutes at the end of class and tell them: *You have worked together today, helping each other do the tasks. It would be nice to thank your partner by writing a positive message especially for him or her.* Give them a special piece of paper, and let them have 5-10 minutes to do this.
Then they stand in a circle, in turns they read out what they have written for their partner, and give the paper to him or her. (See also **A Gift for You**, Activity 5.9.)

CHAPTER 5
A SENSE OF COMPETENCE

Students who feel good about themselves and their abilities are the ones most likely to succeed.

Dr William Purkey

Chapter 5: A Sense of Competence

A feeling of success and accomplishment in areas felt to be important or valuable is a sense of competence. People with a sense of competence take risks, work harder to enjoy more achievement, and have an 'I can do it' spirit based on previous successful experiences that have instilled in them a positive self-image. A sense of competence derives from believing that we can reach our goals, overcome the challenges we face, and make our dreams a reality. **A sense of competence is our confidence in our potential to achieve success.**

Teachers can have a great deal of influence on students' confidence, both in the classroom and beyond. If you as a teacher proactively look for achievement and for your students' good points, you will help to build a sense of competence within them. It is not a question of ignoring what is not well done, but of doing your best to catch students doing something good; when we're learning a new skill, the reward we prize most highly is someone who we respect noticing what we're doing well.

So it is important to acknowledge accomplishment, and not just take it for granted. Verónica remembers how her seventh-grade teacher had her students bring to class little notebooks, and every day during the last five minutes of class she would take the notebooks of two or three students and write a note about something they had done well. Positive feedback from others can help a sense of competence to grow.

Learning well makes students feel competent, and the more competent they feel, the better they learn. Competence involves being responsible and achieving, and it is closely related to happiness.

The Sense of Competence
is knowing that we can reach our goals and be successful.
It requires the ability to:
- identify options available to us.
- apply strategies for problem-solving.
- make good decisions and use our resources well.

Teachers who promote a sense of competence:
- offer options or alternatives.
- provide incentives and support.
- give feedback.
- celebrate achievements.

Suggestions for Building a Sense of Competence

☐ Favourite Work Folder: this is a portfolio kept by students that includes what they feel is their best work. Each week, students choose the work they are proudest of and place it inside their folder. Older students can also be asked to keep track of their own progress with the language by using self-evaluation charts.

- Tape recordings: the purpose here is to allow students to listen to their own progress. Make several recordings of each student throughout the year or term to register their progress in different aspects of spoken English.

- Design a report card where students can record and self-evaluate their own-progress. Teach them to use checklists and progress charts.

- Establish work contracts to increase students' responsibility in keeping track of their progress in academic areas (skills and concepts) and personal development (attitudes).

- When you correct papers, highlight your students' progress. For instance, in written work use a special colour to point out the parts that are especially well written, and write positive comments, such as 'That was a very well presented paper', or 'I was pleased to see the effort you put into the assignment', or 'I am delighted with the story you wrote'. Then, when you need to comment on the parts that need improvement, use 'and' instead of 'but'; for example 'You included some very good ideas, and you can improve your writing if you double-check for spelling errors.'

- Leave a few minutes on the last day of the week for 'Acknowledgement Time'. Give public recognition to students who have done something special that week. Keep track of who you have recognised in this way, so you can be sure to include all students at one time or another. (During the week, whenever you notice someone meriting recognition you could add their name to a list you draw up.) The recognition can be for things such as the following: *I acknowledge you for having helped Marco with his exercise in class ... I acknowledge you for coming to class with your homework prepared ... I acknowledge you for making us laugh one day ... .*

- Keep a notice board to show 'News that makes us happy and proud'

- Create different ways to celebrate success and achievement of goals. Encourage students to discuss ways to celebrate; they could take turns to participate in a Celebration Council.

- Set up different kinds of support for students who might need extra help or extra time to achieve competence in their performance in the target language.

- Help students make more effective use of their time by having them track how they administer their time over a period of two weeks.

- Set up opportunities for students to share the goals they are working on and the progress they are making. Hold little ceremonies to honour those who achieve the goals they have set at the beginning of the quarter.

- Provide continual encouragement for those who need to see that they are making some progress.

- Have a classroom celebration when major class goals have been achieved. This might involve a special movie or a little party.

> **Our sense of competence helps us to overcome obstacles
> and face challenges, to reach our objectives and
> to achieve the success we dream about.
> 'Success breeds Success!'**

5.1 A/B success sharing

Focus: This activity is aimed at giving students a method for focusing on their strengths and counteracting the effects of the inner critic. It promotes a healthy 'can do' spirit in the classroom. It is a good resource for developing listening, speaking and writing skills.

Level: Intermediate +

Time: 10 minutes

Preparation: A stopwatch or other time-keeper.

in class

1. Ask for a volunteer to come up to the front of the room to demonstrate the activity with you. Place two chairs facing each other about an arm's length away from each other, and both of you sit down on them.

2. Explain that one of each pair will be A and the other one will be B; B will speak for about one minute about his/her successes, recent or past. They can use one or several successes – it does not matter how many, or what they are related to. Explain that the purpose of the activity is not to impress the other person; it is simply to be honest and share one success or several with a partner, for one minute. During that minute, while B is sharing, A will listen with full, undivided attention, refraining from commenting, interrupting or finishing the sentence of the other person. When one minute has passed, the students change roles. Demonstrate this with your volunteer, letting him or her choose whether to be A or B.

3. After this demonstration, tell your class that they are now going to do the same with their partners. Ask As to raise their hands, and then say that Bs will start sharing. Keep track of time; when one minute has passed, ask them to change roles.

Extension
As a follow-up activity, you can invite students to share something their partner said about their successful experiences. You can also ask your students to write about the success story they shared with the partner, but now in more detail.

Variation
Another option is to have them start a Success Log (see Activity 5.5) or build a Success Corner in the classroom. If possible in your context, you can create a Success Corner with a notice board where students can post short notes about their successes. It will encourage them to participate if you post a success of yours first.

Acknowledgement
The idea for this activity came from Jack Canfield.

5.2 Words have power!

Focus: To give students a sense of competence by promoting a 'can do' spirit in the classroom. Also, this activity is a powerful tool to make students aware that words have power, and it complements **Words that open, Words that close**, Activity 1.10.

Level: Intermediate +

Time: 40-50 minutes

Preparation: Draw up a list of some things you feel you can't do and would like to do.

in class

1. Start the class by putting this statement on the board: **Words have Power**. Have them get into small groups and discuss it. Ask for a few ideas and then help them explore the idea more by giving them the following questions to think about:

   > **WORDS HAVE POWER**
   >
   > What happens when you say 'I can't do it!'
   > What happens when you say 'I'll do my best.'
   > What happens when you say 'It's too hard!'
   > What happens when you say 'What if ...'
   > What happens when you say 'I should / I have to ...'
   > What happens when you say 'I want to ...'
   > What happens when you say 'I'm going to ...'

2. Give your students around 10-15 minutes to talk about this, and then ask them to choose a representative of each group to share their ideas. While they are doing this, you can act as a scribe, making a mind map of the main points presented. (If you're unfamiliar with mind maps, check Activity 2.5.)

3. Tell each student to write down some things they feel **they can't do and** they **would like to do**. As they write, give out a strip of paper to each student. After about 5 minutes tell them to choose one item from their list, e.g. 'I can't dance', and write it down on the strip of paper. Tell them to fold that strip of paper several times (you also do this with one item from your list), and then tell them to tear it into many pieces. Allow a few moments of fun. Then ask them to replace that limiting statement with an empowering one such as 'I can learn to dance' or 'I can develop my ability to dance'.

4. Have them take the remaining 'can't' statements on their list and cross them out and replace them with positive ones, and then invite them to share with the whole class some of their favourites.

5.2 Words have power!

Extension
As a follow-up, have them write these phrases and then complete each sentence.
- ☐ **One of my achievements is ...**
- ☐ **Something I am good at is ...**
- ☐ **Something I am going to learn is ...**

Make time for students to read out their favourite completion to the class, using the 'hot potato' technique (see Activity 3.10). And ... enjoy it! You will see how the 'can do' spirit in the classroom raises the energy of the whole class, including your own.

5.3 Turning points: connecting the dots

Focus: Speaking and writing. To show students how competence is often achieved by facing challenges or difficulties that at first appear as major obstacles.

Level: Upper intermediate +

Time: 50 minutes

Preparation: Make a photocopy of each of Pictures 1 and 2 below, or have them on your computer to project for the class.
Video of Steve Jobs from the internet:
http://www.youtube.com/watch?v=D1R-jKKp3NA&hl=es.
Alternatively, bring a written biography of an inspiring person; Steve Jobs' speech can be found by searching on "transcript Steve Jobs Stanford speech".
Optional: think about the turning points in your own life, and list them, ready to discuss with the students.
A copy of the worksheet for each student.
Bring in a CD player to play Track 11 on the CD or some quiet music to read to.

in class

1. Show Picture 1; the students shout out what they think it is. Then show them Picture 2 (with the dots joined), explaining how important moments in our lives can, when connected, form a picture of who we are.

2. If you have access to the internet in the classroom, you can show your students the empowering video about Steve Jobs, creator of Apple Computers, where he talks about connecting the dots in life. If you do not have internet access in the classroom, you can tell your students about the life of someone like Nelson Mandela, Martin Luther King, Anne Frank, Oprah Winfrey, Gandhi, or anyone who could be inspiring and who you feel your students could relate to. Or if you prefer, you could hand out a written biography for them to read. Ask your students to make a note of the major events in the person's life, especially the 'turning points' (moments in life when a dramatic change takes place).

3. Students compare notes in pairs. Then invite the whole class to participate in a discussion which includes questions such as:
   - Which were the major turning points and/or major events in the life of this person?
   - How do you think these events affected him/her?
   - Can you think of other examples of turning points in the life of a person you know or know of?

   At this point it would be very positive for the class if you also use the example of the turning points in your own life.

5.3 Turning points: connecting the dots

4. After this introduction, you can do a guided visualisation with them, in order to help them to find the turning points/major events of their own lives. Play the CD, or play your music and say:
*Close your eyes and simply focus on your breathing ... (pause for 5–10 seconds between each phrase) ... observe how you inhale ... and exhale ... slowly and gently ... Now go back in time ... and allow images, feelings, memories related to major events in your life to appear ... Remember and see in your mind ...
... a time when you had to struggle to overcome an obstacle
... a time when you were scared at first, and then you had fun
... a moment in your life when you were afraid of doing something new
... a time you enjoyed doing something new
... a time of uncertainty that later on turned into something exciting
... a major discovery
... a major decision
... a major choice.
Now, start focusing on your breathing again ... observe how you inhale ... exhale ... slowly, gently ... in ... out ... and whenever you are ready, gently open your eyes and return to this room.*
Give each student the worksheet and let them spend about 15 minutes writing down anything they remember from the visualisation or that pops into their mind as they write.

A time when you had to struggle to overcome an obstacle

A time when you where scared at first and then you found it was fun

A moment in your life when you were afraid of doing something new

A time you enjoyed doing something new

A time of uncertainty that later on turned into something exciting

A major discovery

A major decision

A major choice

5.3 Turning points: connecting the dots

5. Then ask them to choose just one of these turning points and share it with the person next to them.

Extension
For a follow-up, either in class or as homework, students can write a composition connecting these turning points.

Variations
1. Using an interactive whiteboard, copy Picture 1 onto a page. After students try to guess what it is, have a student come to the board and join the dots to check if they were right.

2. In Step 2, narrating the life of an inspiring person; if you have an interactive whiteboard, you could cut and paste photos from the internet about the person's life on separate pages, and under each photo write a sentence which summarises the turning point – then hide this sentence at first. As you mention the important points of their life, show the related photos. When you finish, show the photos again, and ask students to give a summary of each turning point; then reveal your summary.

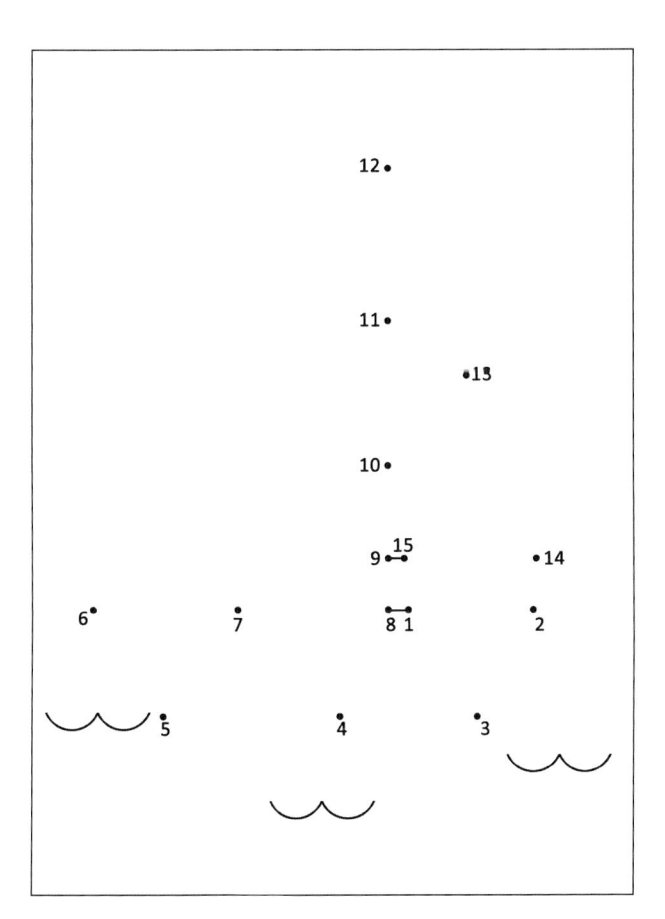

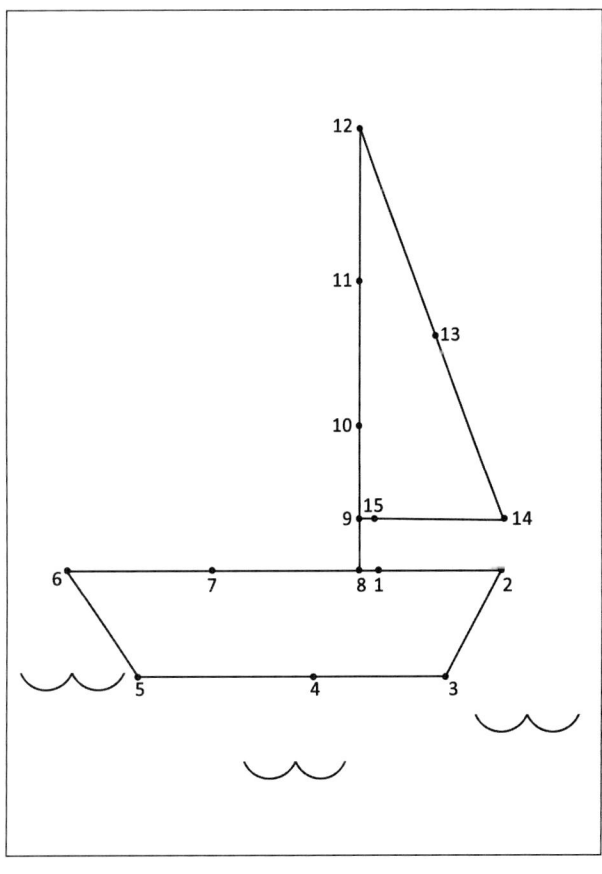

CHAPTER 5: A SENSE OF COMPETENCE 151

5.4 What I know

Focus: Reading and writing.

Level: Lower intermediate +

Time: Part of several class periods

Preparation: A copy of the Fulghum text (at the end of this activity) for each student.
Bring in a CD player to play Track 12 on the CD or some music you can read to, that fits with the text.

in class

1. Have students brainstorm important things that they have learned in life. Give them a few examples of things you have learned: *To speak ... To read ... To help my friends ....* Tell them the things don't have to be big or unusual.
Give them a few minutes to write some things, and then ask them to share some of these.

2. Tell them they are going to listen to a text about what one writer learned. Tell them they don't have to understand everything or even most of it; they just listen. Either play the CD, or else read the text aloud while playing your own music, with your voice following it.

3. Ask them for any words or phrases they remember. Hand out the text, and explain a few things they might not understand[1]. Then they read it on their own, silently.

4. When they have finished, for a third reading go around the room and have each student read one line/sentence. To finish the text, you may have to go around more than once.

5. Tell the class that they are going to write their own texts on the topic 'What I know'. This will give them the opportunity to reflect on what they have learned that is important for their lives. They can follow the text as a model if they wish, adapting it to fit their experience.
For this writing project, use the Writing Process Technique, which consists of the following steps:

---

[1] The 'Dick and Jane' books were a series of books used in the USA for teaching children how to read; 'blankies' are blankets, and 'Sunday School' refers to classes of religious education and entertainment on Sundays for children at some churches. The Golden Rule is: 'Do unto others as you would have them do unto you'.

5.4 What I know

> A Pre-writing: brainstorming ideas while thinking about examples of good writing.
>
> B Drafting: preparation of the initial text. At this stage they can also check for clarity and style, discussing with peers and teacher.
>
> C Editing: checking the draft for spelling, grammar and punctuation, and producing a final version.
>
> D Publishing: sharing the written work with others.

6. For the rest of that first lesson, let them tackle the pre-writing stage.

Homework/Lesson 2 onwards

7. Assign the drafting for homework, or allow some time to work in the next class.
   For the editing, you could pick up their work and check it – but you might prefer to put them into groups of 3 or 4 for them to read each other's texts and make any suggestions they might have.
   When they have a final copy ready, they could illustrate it with any drawings or pictures they can find, related to what they have written.
   Finally find a way to publish. Some possibilities would be to display on the classroom walls for everyone to be able to read, make a little book with photocopies of all the texts, put the stories on the school web site or create a special blog for them.

Note
The publishing stage is very important, as the students' feeling of competence is supported when something they have done is seen and appreciated by others. And as Wright and Hill (2008:11) say, publishing develops 'in the students' minds the idea that they are responsible for communicating their ideas to other people and are not merely submitting writing in English for the teacher to mark'.

5.4 What I know

All I Really Need To Know I Learned In Kindergarten by Robert Fulghum

ALL I REALLY NEED TO KNOW about how to live and what to do and how to be I learned in kindergarten. Wisdom was not at the top of the graduate-school mountain, but there in the sandpile at Sunday School. These are the things I learned:
Share everything.
Play fair.
Don't hit people.
Put things back where you found them.
Clean up your own mess.
Don't take things that aren't yours.
Say you're sorry when you hurt somebody.
Wash your hands before you eat.
Flush.
Warm cookies and cold milk are good for you.
Live a balanced life – learn some and think some and draw and paint and sing and dance and play and work every day some.
Take a nap every afternoon.
When you go out into the world, watch out for traffic, hold hands, and stick together.
Be aware of wonder.
Remember the little seed in the styrofoam cup: the roots go down and the plant goes up, and nobody really knows how or why, but we are all like that.
Goldfish and hamsters and white mice and even the little seed in the Styrofoam cup - they all die.
So do we.
And then remember the Dick-and-Jane books and the first word you learned – the biggest word of all – LOOK.
Everything you need to know is in there somewhere.
The Golden Rule and love and basic sanitation.
Ecology and politics and equality and sane living.
Take any of those items and extrapolate it into sophisticated adult terms and apply it to your family life or your work or your government or your world, and it holds true and clear and firm.
Think what a better world it would be if all - the whole world - had cookies and milk about three o'clock every afternoon and then lay down with our blankies for a nap. Or if all governments had a basic policy to always put things back where they found them and to clean up their own mess.
And it is still true, no matter how old you are – when you go out into the world, it is best to hold hands and stick together.

5.5 My success log

Focus: Writing and speaking. To activate your students' sense of achievement, make them aware of what they do well, and learn to acknowledge themselves and others for their achievements.

Level: Lower intermediate +

Time: Variable

Preparation: Bring in a CD player to play Track 6 on the CD or some other inspiring music.

in class

1. Tell your students to bring a little notebook to class, one they really like, because this will be a special place where they will keep a record of their successes. It is important that you, as role model, also keep this success log and bring it to share with them when you want to begin this activity, which can be used as a routine. They can write every day if they want to, so they need the log handy.
Stress that these do not have to be great achievements; they can be things like 'I heard someone speak in English on television and I could understand part of what they said' or on a personal level 'I stayed calm when my friend was criticising me' ...

2. Periodically you can have a special time - a Success Celebration - for sharing what they have written. For the Success Celebration, ask students to sit in a circle, then play the music, and allow them to take turns sharing one or two entries from their Success Log. The rules are the following:
   - You speak only when it's your turn.
   - No comments on what others say.
   You can also use this rule if you wish:
   - When someone finishes sharing, the class responds, *Thank you for sharing.*
   Depending on the time available, all students who would like to participate can do so, or you can say that you have time for five or seven volunteers. When they want to participate, they put up their hands, and they speak one at a time.

Note
A Success Log is a useful way to get students to improve their self-talk, and thus their self-image. It is also a very powerful tool to dilute fear when they have something to do that might be anxiety-provoking, such as taking an important exam. They can go back to their log to review their past achievements, which can give them the confidence they need at the current moment. We have found that sometimes it is easier for learners to write and talk about their successes in a foreign language; it is as if doing it in a foreign language lets them be free from old patterns of negative thinking.

5.6 Appreciation works!

Focus: To enhance your students' sense of competence, by focusing on appreciation and acknowledgement.

Level: Lower intermediate +

Time: 40-50 minutes

Preparation: None.

in class

1. Start your class by talking with your students about the importance of appreciation and acknowledgement; see note below.

2. Students jot down their answers to the following questions individually, and then discuss them as a class:
   - What is appreciation?
   - Do you think it is important? Why?

3. After the class discussion, they form groups to answer the following question:
   - How can we express appreciation?

   They brainstorm different possibilities for activities that can be done in the classroom to express appreciation; they can also extend the idea and come up with suggestions to express appreciation for the whole school and their families. Ask each group to choose the three ideas they like the best and write them on a piece of paper. Give them approximately 10-15 minutes to complete this step.

4. Next, ask one member of each group to present those ideas to the rest of the class. When all ideas have been presented, pick up the papers from each group so that for the next class you can write them all in an attractive way on a poster to display in class.

Extension

As a follow-up, the students could do an Appreciation Project in the school. This could include an Appreciation Book and a mural.

Prepare a special large notebook where they can write down notes in English about people or things that they appreciate, related to the school. You might make this book yourself out of sheets of different coloured paper.

If it is kept where anyone in the school can read it, teachers who don't know much English may want you to help translate things so they can see what is being written in the book.

Then for a mural on large sheets of paper, have students in groups interview different people in the school - these can include not just the Director or Head of Studies but others as well; encourage your

5.6 Appreciation works!

students to interview the cleaning person, someone who works in the school cafeteria etc. These interviews would be presented on the mural bilingually in English and in the language of the community so that everyone can read them, and would include at the end of each some words of appreciation and possibly photos.

Note
Learning to express and receive appreciation is perhaps one of the most powerful attitudes to be developed in order to create a sense of competence in your students and build a positive environment in your classroom. And remember, when you feel competent it is easy to appreciate others.

Acknowledgement
Thanks to Inmaculada León, who told us about a similar project at the secondary school where she teaches in Azuaga, Spain.

5.7 A letter of acknowledgement

Focus: Learning to express acknowledgement in writing. You may like to do this after **Appreciation works!**, Activity 5.6.

Level: Intermediate +

Time: 40-50 minutes

Preparation: Make photocopies of the worksheet and model letter, or write these on the board. Write the quotation below on the board.

in class

1. Begin by asking your class to copy this quotation from the board:

> *There is more hunger for love and appreciation in this world than for bread.* (Mother Teresa, Nobel Peace Prize 1979)

    Ask your students to write one thing that the quotation means to them, and then several or all students read what they have written. Then have a whole-class discussion around the quotation.

2. Review (unless you have done this in a recent class) the conventions of informal letter writing, and tell your students that it is important to acknowledge others who have done something for us. It is important both for them and for us, so now they are going to write a letter of acknowledgement.

3. Start by asking them to think of one person in their life they would like to thank. To help them think of someone, invite them to close their eyes for minute, in order to concentrate. You can guide them by using the following words:
   Who has made a difference in your life? ... One person that made you feel confident ... someone who has believed in you ... someone who has encouraged you in times of trouble ... someone who has helped you go through a hard time of your life ... someone who made a difference in your life ...

4. Allow a few moments, and then tell them to open their eyes. Distribute the following worksheet with guiding questions, or write it on the board:

5.7 A letter of acknowledgement

> 1. Who would you like to acknowledge today?
>
> 2. What did that person do for you? (Be very specific.)
>
> 3. In what way has your life been enriched by this person's action or attitude?
>
> 4. When you write them a letter of acknowledgement, how would you like to end your letter?

To begin to write the letter, they can use this model (add any other expressions you feel would be useful). Walk around the class and help them with language they may need as they write.

> 1. Introduction. 'Today I want to thank you for …'
> 2. Describe the way that person has made you feel: 'I feel supported by …'
> 3. Describe how this was important for you: 'I want to tell you that my life…'
> 4. If this has influenced how you will act, you can write: 'As a result of this, I …'
> 5. Ending. Example: 'I will remember …'

Note
This activity is one where it is the doing, and not the product, that is important, so we recommend not having students hand in the letter to be corrected. You have helped them with any doubts as they write, and the language learning is supported in this part of the activity. Instead, you could suggest that they keep the letter to read at some point in the future, or perhaps they might like to actually give it to the person they are acknowledging, translating it to their L1 if this person doesn't read English.
If you want to have a closing to the activity in the classroom, go around the room and have each student say in a brief sentence who they wanted to thank and why, without going into details as in the letter itself.

5.8 The attitude of gratitude

Focus: Writing and speaking. Learning to feel and express gratitude is a very important life skill that enables us function at our best. This activity is aimed at teaching your students to acknowledge people in their life for their support, loving attitudes and caring gestures. It is also a way to build strong bonds between the students; it gives them the opportunity to focus on the positive qualities they possess and reinforce a positive self-image of each other.
This activity is to be done late enough in the term for students to know each other fairly well.

Level: Intermediate +

Time: 20 minutes

Preparation: Bring in one small blank white card for each student, and a CD player to play Track 13 on the CD or some soft, relaxing music.

in class

1. Begin your class by brainstorming with your students what the concept of appreciation means to them or, alternatively, do this after **Appreciation Works!** (Activity 5.6). Write down what they say on the board, and you can also add your own thoughts. Then you can say that even if the concept is important, very often we forget to put it into practice, because we take people for granted, and silent appreciation is not of much use to anyone! Tell them that today you are going to take them on a trip to a land called *Gratitude* and for them to relax and not worry if they don't understand everything you say – just to let the words touch them.

2. Tell your students to sit in a comfortable position and close their eyes if they want. Ask them to become aware of their breathing. Play the CD, or play your music and say the following words slowly in a calm voice, pausing after each line:

   > *Take a few deep breaths.*
   > *There are people in our life who make us feel valued and respected ...*
   > *who remember what we do right and forget what we do wrong ...*
   > *who appreciate us without judging ...*
   > *who join us without invading ...*
   > *who invite us without demanding ...*
   > *People who help us grow by showing us the next mountain to climb or a new path to explore ...*
   > *People who show us the way when we are lost ...*
   > *People who sing our song when we forget the lines ...*
   > *People who love us with no conditions attached ...*
   > *People who respect our space to develop, to shine, to do our best...*

5.8 The attitude of gratitude

3. When you have finished this part, tell your students to take a few deep breaths, gently open their eyes, and come back to the classroom space.

4. Now, in the appreciation mode, the next step is to express appreciation to each other in the following way:
   - Give out a card to each student, and ask them to write their name on it.
   - Collect all the cards, and shuffle them.
   - Put them in the centre of the classroom, all facing down, and invite each student to take one card. Ask the students not to show anyone the name they got.
   - Then tell them to think of that person, and consider at least one specific action that person can be acknowledged for; and also consider things that person may be good at, or admired for. You may want to stress that the rule of the game is no matter whose name you have, you find something good to say about that person.
   - Tell them to write down, on the other side of the card, the list of qualities or actions that they want to appreciate that person for. Since the card is small, even a short list will do. Or it can be one good thing they find, explained in some detail.
   - When they finish writing the card, ask them to give the card to the person they wrote about. And allow a few moments of free exchange.
   - Finish the class by making a circle, allowing each student to say a few words about what they feel after the experience, even one word to close the activity is fine.

5.9 A gift for you

Focus: Language for giving and receiving. This is a good activity to do in the second half of a lesson after students have been working in pairs on a fairly demanding exercise that has required a lot of attention and cooperation, or after the whole class has worked hard and successfully on a project or on mastering a new grammar point, etc. This activity is a nice way to celebrate an accomplishment, even a small one.

Level: Elementary +

Time: 20–25 minutes

Preparation: Copy and paste the slide to a page on an interactive whiteboard. Otherwise, you can project it on the computer and/or write the words for the five senses on the blackboard.
In a previous lesson, review or present typical language used for giving and receiving gifts.

in class

1. Have your students look at the five categories that you have projected or written on the blackboard. Then ask them first to think of things they like **seeing**. You can add these to the board, or they can come up and write their suggestions on the interactive whiteboard or blackboard. Then go on to things they like hearing, touching, smelling and tasting, one by one. Stop when you have several suggestions for each category, and then erase all the suggestions.

2. Put the students into pairs, and tell them it would be nice to give each other a gift. Ask the As to think of their partner and decide on one thing under each sensory category that they would like to give them; they can use some of the things mentioned before, but encourage them to think of some others too.

3. Ask Bs to close their eyes if they want, and to imagine what their gifts are like as their partner gives them. As will use any language they know for giving gifts, but will begin by using their partner's name. They should pause to give the Bs time to enjoy each sensory gift before giving the next one. For example:
Lucia, I have something special I would like to give you (I have a little present for you; I hope you like it …). I want you to see a cat playing with a ball … I want you to hear rain on the roof … I want you to touch velvet … I want you to smell bread baking … I want you to taste pizza.
Then the Bs open their eyes and, using their partner's name, thank the As:
Mario, thank you so much for the presents. I really liked them (Thank you for the wonderful presents …).

5.9 A gift for you

4. Now they change roles, and Bs give the sensory gifts to As.

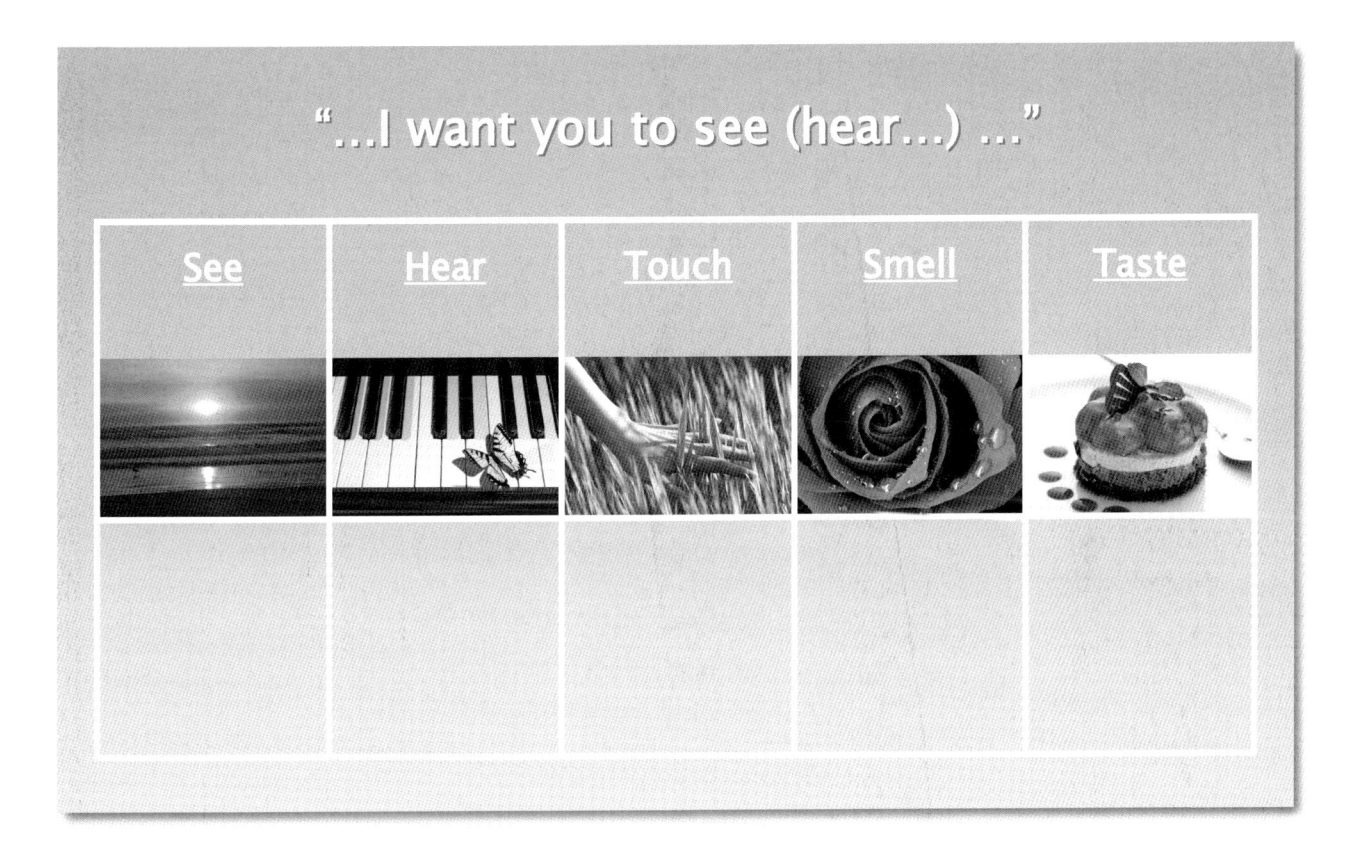

"...I want you to see (hear...) ..."

See	Hear	Touch	Smell	Taste

Acknowledgement
This activity was inspired by one in Arnold, Puchta and Rinvolucri's *Imagine That! Mental Imagery in the EFL Classroom*, 2007 (Helbling Languages).

Variation
To review the language learned another day, you can put students in pairs and tell the class *It is our birthday today. All of us have a birthday. We are going to give each other a special present.* Explain that they are each going to think of their partner and what they might like to receive as a gift, and then – being careful that their partner can't see what they are doing – they will draw a picture of it and fold up the paper, maybe drawing a ribbon or a design like wrapping paper on the outside. When both have finished, A will give the 'present' to B, using some of the language of giving that they have learned, and B will open the present and thank A. Then B gives, and A thanks.

5.10 A happy day!

Focus: Writing and speaking about an experience in the past. To enhance your students' sense of competence by focusing on a happy moment that was very meaningful to them, and allowing them to share this with their classmates. This activity also lets them practise listening to each other.

Level: Intermediate +

Time: 15 minutes

Preparation: Make one copy of the worksheet for each student. Ensure you have a stopwatch, or something to time one minute. Optional; hand bell.

in class

1. Tell your students to relax and think of a time at school, at home or elsewhere – a special moment, when they felt really good about themselves. It can be recent or many years ago. When they have had time to think of the moment, continue by asking them the questions in the worksheet as a guided visualisation, saying them in a calm voice and giving the students time to activate in their minds the images of the moment.

2. Then give each student the worksheet to fill in. At this point you can help them with any language they need.

3. When they have completed this part of the activity, they put away the worksheets and form groups of 5 or 6. Tell them that each will have 1 minute to share with the others in their group their memories of their Happy Day. It is very important to tell them that when one person is speaking, the others will be listening only.

4. All groups should start at the same time, so ask them to decide who is going to be first, and then tell them that you will indicate when to start (e.g. ring a bell, or clap your hands), and when to change.
Each member of the group will be given one minute to talk, and when their time is up, the person to the left will begin; this will be repeated until the last person has spoken.

5. When all have shared, you can give them a few minutes to allow them to ask each other any questions or make any comments.

5.10 A happy day!

> Thinking of that day and time when you felt really good about yourself – When was it?
>
> Where did it happen?
>
> What happened?
>
> Who was with you?
>
> How did you feel?
>
> What did you do that made you feel that way?

5.11 The magic minute

Focus: To develop speaking competence and give your students a chance to talk in front of a group. This activity is a comfortable way to engage in self-disclosure. It is aimed at creating a feeling of competence for everyone in the classroom, which leads to an optimal climate for language learning. The message is that we all have something to feel proud of, to feel grateful for. This is an activity to do after the class has been together for some time.

Level: Lower intermediate +

Time: Lesson 1, 5–10 minutes; 20–25 minutes if you use the Variation; Lesson 2, depends on the size of your class – a minute or two per student – or with the Variation about 10 minutes.

Preparation: For Lesson 2, an object that represents a positive moment for you.

in class

Lesson 1

1. Tell your students that for the next class they are supposed to bring with them an object that represents a positive moment for them, something they feel proud of and grateful for. Give a few examples: photos, letters, objects in general. The important thing here is that the object is the starting point for them to prepare a one-minute speech about what the object stands for. The moment doesn't have to be about something major; for example, someone might feel proud of having helped a friend pass a difficult exam, and if the exam paper itself is not available they could bring in a sheet of paper where they wrote the mark the friend got for the exam.

2. It may be easier for them to organise their minute if you give them the following questions to ponder:
   - What is the object?
   - Who gave it to you, or how did you get it?
   - Why is it important to you?

Lesson 2

3. Invite your students to form a circle. You should also participate in this activity; by being the first to speak, you make it easier for the students themselves to open up.

4. Holding your object in your hand, talk about it for a minute. You may ask someone to volunteer to keep time. When the minute is over, the student next to you will continue; and the same until all students have had a chance to speak. It is very important to tell them not to clap or comment or interrupt when someone else is presenting, even after the speech. Tell them *The rule is to remain silent and listening until it is your turn.* This way you are creating

5.11 The magic minute

a safe environment, built on care and mutual respect. This is an activity that generates a lot of interest and closeness between members of the group.

Variation
If you have large classes or if it is early in the course and the students don't know each other well yet, for Lesson 1 when you assign the Magic Minute talks, you might want to do the following: divide students into groups of 5 and give them 2 minutes in silence to think about a topic that would be appropriate for them (something they would really like to do in the future, values that are important for them, something nice that they remember from their childhood …) or simply have them each say two things about themselves. Then they go around the circle and say anything they want to about the topic or about themselves. When they have finished, assign the talks for Lesson 2, on the following day. Tell your students that they will give their talk to the same group they have worked with. Students who are very reticent to speak in front of the whole class find it easier to speak this way.

5.12 It's your choice

Focus: Autonomy brings with it a sense of competence. A key element in developing autonomous behaviour in students is to give them choice. On a very basic level, we can ask a class if they want to do one activity that we have planned first, or another one – or we can let them do an exercise individually or with the person next to them. Even though we may have to follow the syllabus closely, there is always room for some choice.

Level: Elementary +

Time: Variable

Preparation: See the different suggestions below.

in class

One way to build in choice from time to time is to let each student choose what they want to do as homework on a text we have dealt with in class. This may seem a bit disorganised, and it does involve more work for us teachers than merely reading out the correct answers for exercises in the textbook – but even used only occasionally, it can come as great relief for both students and for teachers, and can motivate students and provide them with a sense of accomplishment.

For example, if we have read a story in class, we could let our students pick an option such as one of the following, to be presented to the class the following day:

- ☐ Choose your favourite character in the story. Explain why you like him/her. Write three questions that you would like to ask him/her, and the answers you think he/she would give.

- ☐ Make a list of positive attitudes of the characters. Circle the one that is most important to you. You can use this information to make an advertisement for this attitude, as if you were trying to persuade people to buy it.

- ☐ Choose your favourite scene/s in the story, and find someone who would like to roleplay that scene with you. Prepare this for the next class.

- ☐ Are you happy with the way the author ended the story? Explain why.
  Would you like to write a different ending? If so, how would it be?

- ☐ Write a sentence from the story that was really meaningful to you. Complete this statement 'It was meaningful to me because ...' Make a poster with that sentence.

5.12 It's your choice

- ☐ Think of two or three new words that you learned from the story. Write them down and put them in your 'treasure word box'. Write a letter to a friend and include these words.

- ☐ Have you ever felt like the main character in the story? Write about that experience.

- ☐ How did you feel throughout the story? Think of the scenes that impressed you the most. Write about some of those scenes, making reference to your feelings and explaining them.

- ☐ Express the main idea(s) of the story in another format: a poem, a song, an essay, a drawing …

Variation
The above suggestions would be appropriate for intermediate level and above, but other ideas could be found for elementary students. For example, they could memorise a simple poem they have read, and with a classmate prepare a dramatic recitation; modify the poem by adding a few more words; using the basic structure of the poem, create a new poem; put the poem to music and sing it, etc.

5.13 Ping pong of talents

Focus: To review the structure *To be good at* + the *-ing* form of a verb.
To reinforce students' feeling of competence in other areas of their lives, which can influence their beliefs about their abilities regarding language learning.

Level: Lower intermediate +

Time: 10–15 minutes

Preparation: Optional; bring in a pair of puppets. Stopwatch or other device to time a minute. Optional; hand bell.

in class

1. Remind students that all of us are good at a lot of things, and that they don't have to be big things to be important in our lives. Explain to your students that they are going to remember some of these now. To give them examples, tell them some things you are good at (listening to friends, gardening, baking cakes ...). Give them a few moments to think of some things they can do well, whether they are small things or very significant ones. They don't write these – just think for a little while.

2. Demonstrate the activity with a student (or use two puppets and invent their 'talents'). For one minute, you tell the other person as many things as you can that you do well, each one beginning with *I am good at ..., I am good at ...*. Stress that they need to use the *-ing* form after the expression 'good at'. After the minute is over, the student who was listening repeats back what their partner was good at, repeating before each point *You are good at ..., You are good at ...* .

3. Get students into pairs, and ask them to stand up. The As raise their hands and you then tell your students that the Bs will begin speaking first. At the end of a minute, ring a bell or clap your hands, and As repeat back what Bs are good at. After another minute, stop and give As their minute to say what they are good at. Finally, Bs repeat back to As. Control the time carefully.

Extension
As a follow-up, if you wish, your students stand in a circle, and each person says one thing that their partner is good at.

Variation
If you have an interactive whiteboard*, you can play **Guess what I'm good at**; for homework beforehand, students find at least four or five images that are related in some way to things they are good at. It is better if the images chosen do not have too obvious a connection with one another. Your students email their images to you, and you

5.13 Ping pong of talents

can paste each student's images on a different page.

In class, one student begins by saying 'Guess what I'm good at!' and the rest of the class looks at the images on the page; when the class guesses one correctly, the student erases the image. If any are too difficult to guess, the student can give hints. After all images are gone, you can have someone try to remember all the things and say, *You are good at ..., you are good at ..., you are good at ... and you are good at ....*

* If an interactive whiteboard isn't available you can still play it; students could bring in drawings they have made or photos from magazines, one to a page.

5.14 My strengths

Focus: Review the lexical area of personal qualities. The aim of this activity is to help your students focus on their strengths and on the strengths of others. Becoming more aware of strengths provides support for developing competence.
This is an activity to use later on in the course, when students know each other well enough to be able to comment on each other's strengths.

Level: Lower intermediate +

Time: 30–45 minutes

Preparation: Make a copy of the worksheet for each student. Bring in a CD player to play Track 8 on the CD or some other soft music. Optional: hand bell.

in class

1. Divide the class into groups of 5 or 6, sitting in circles; try to group students who feel comfortable with each other. Explain that you are going to do an activity that will allow them to focus on their strengths, to become more aware of their positive qualities in order to use them even more effectively.

2. Give each student a copy of the worksheet; tell them to write their name. Then they write positive qualities they see in themselves in the inner circle: these can be about the way they relate to others, or things they are good at, or anything they like about themselves. Give them around 5–10 minutes to do this, check whether they have completed this part of the task, and allow one more minute if someone hasn't finished.

3. Next, tell them to pass the sheet to their left, so that each student can write down in part of the outer circle a few things he or she likes or admires about that person. Tell them that the other members of their group will also be writing in the outer circle. Give them 2 minutes per student. To control the time, you can ring the bell, or say 'Next!'

4. Continue doing this until all the students have had a chance to complete the outer circle for all members of the group, adding each time to the list of strengths they see in each other.

5. The students receive back their own worksheet, with the outside circle completed. While you play the music, they can read what their classmates have written, and then have a moment for reflection and self-awareness. Tell them that only when you have stopped the music may anyone talk.

Acknowledgement
Verónica learned this activity at Jack Canfield's FSS training, 1999.

5.14 My strengths

MY STRENGTHS

Name: _____

APPENDIX

Appendix: Going Beyond

As teachers, one of our most important goals should be to become more autonomous. We do this when we develop more resources, and one of the advantages of resource books is precisely this; that they can help us to gain more autonomy.

However, not all activities you see in this or any other book are going to be perfect for all contexts. It is very important to keep in mind your students' and your own preferences. Often, for an activity to be successful the best procedure is not to **adopt** it directly from a book but rather to **adapt** it to our own situation. As you look through the activities here, we encourage you to make any changes that you think would make them better for your students. When considering any activity, keep in mind your students' needs, the way you feel comfortable teaching, and techniques that you have used before successfully, all of which might give you ideas for adapting all or part of an activity. In this way, our activities become fully yours.

Learning – which is what, in a sense, gives us greater autonomy – can be considered to rest on two bases: experience and reflection.

LEARNING/ AUTONOMY	
experience	reflection

We gain experience automatically every time we walk into our classroom; but if it is going to serve us for growing professionally, we also need to incorporate reflection. This involves going back to experience, remembering both what happened and how we felt in as much detail as possible, trying to find multiple explanations for whatever happened, and then generating ways to make improvements in future situations of a similar nature.

One useful tool for reflective practitioners is keeping a teaching journal in which we record ideas and options we have considered and/or done. When you are using any of these activities, we recommend you make notes after class; the greater the involvement with what we are doing, the more effective we will be.

In order to arrive at the clearest idea possible of how an activity went, it is very helpful to ask those involved. While avoiding routine questioning and therefore routine response, we can still get a lot of feedback from our students. Sometimes, carefully

Appendix: Going Beyond

observing their reactions is enough; at other times we can ask a few questions: *Did you enjoy this activity? What did you like about it? Anything you would change?* ... Or maybe a quick show of hands to see how many would rate the activity as a 3 (liked it), 2 (so-so) or 1 (didn't like it much).

It is also good to remember that there is strength in numbers. If we join with other teachers to discuss what has worked for us, and share photocopies and other materials that can be reused, we all benefit.

Finally, you may find some useful information for reflection by completing, in a spirit of exploration and discovery, the following teacher self-evaluation forms, based on the five components of Reasoner's model of self-esteem.

TEACHER'S SELF-EVALUATION: ESTABLISHING A SENSE OF SECURITY

	ALMOST ALWAYS	USUALLY	SOME-TIMES	SELDOM or NEVER
1. Do I respect the personal rights of my students, and ensure that the personal rights of each student are protected in the classroom?				
2. Do I communicate to my students that I feel they are important as individuals?				
3. Do I clearly define the rules I expect students to follow in the classroom?				
4. Do I help my students to develop a sense of individual responsibility?				
5. Do I project an image that tells the students I am here to build and support rather than to criticise?				
6. Do I find ways to demonstrate my faith and trust in my students?				
7. Do I avoid disciplining or embarrassing students in front of their peers?				
8. Do I provide positive reinforcement for students when they comply with the rules?				
9. Do I make provisions for my students to grow in self-control?				
10. Do I enforce rules and expectations in ways that build positive self-images rather than negative ones?				

Subtotals

$\times 4 =$ ___ $+ \times 3 =$ ___ $+ \times 2 =$ ___ $+ \times 1 =$ ___

37 – 40 = Super!!!
32 – 36 = Excellent!!
27 – 31 = Good!
22 – 26 = Fair
<22 = I need to work at this

Total _____

How to calculate your total:
1. Add the points in each column, and write their sum on the Subtotals line.
2. For the Almost Always column, multiply your subtotal by 4 and write the answer in the space after the = sign.
3. For the other 3 columns, do the same, but multiplying your subtotal by 3, 2 or 1, as shown.
4. Add the four numbers you've just written, and insert their sum as the Total.

TEACHER'S SELF-EVALUATION: ESTABLISHING A SENSE OF IDENTITY

	ALMOST ALWAYS	USUALLY	SOME-TIMES	SELDOM or NEVER
1. Do I let my students know in some way that I am interested in each of them as a unique person?				
2. Do I provide time for students to talk with me on a semiprivate basis?				
3. Do I make a point of talking with individual students on topics not directly related to their academic work?				
4. Do I convey an attitude of warmth and personal concern for my students?				
5. Can I identify some strengths of each student?				
6. Do I notice and comment on things that are important to my students?				
7. Do I show students who return from an absence that they were missed?				
8. Do I give students information about skills needs in ways that build positive rather than negative feelings?				
9. Do I help my students discover their strengths and their points for development?				
10. Do I reinforce students' positive attributes?				

Subtotals   ___   ___   ___   ___

× 4= ___ + × 3= ___ +× 2= ___ + × 1= ___

37 – 40 = Super!!!
32 – 36 = Excellent!!
27 – 31 = Good!
22 – 26 = Fair
   <22 = I need to work at this

Total _____

TEACHER'S SELF-EVALUATION: ESTABLISHING A SENSE OF BELONGING

	ALMOST ALWAYS	USUALLY	SOME-TIMES	SELDOM or NEVER
1. Do I create a climate of acceptance and confidence in the classroom?				
2. Do I use activities that help students get to know each other?				
3. Do I provide opportunities to develop group pride?				
4. Do I make an effort to include students who may feel isolated?				
5. Do I help students acquire the social skills of being a friend, working cooperatively and being sensitive to the needs of others?				
6. Do I plan activities that foster team or class cohesiveness?				
7. Do I express pride in students directly to them?				
8. Do I provide opportunities for students to gain peer recognition for their efforts and achievements?				
9. Do I provide opportunities for students to work together cooperatively?				
10. Do I discourage students from ridiculing or rejecting others?				

Subtotals   ___ ___ ___ ___

× 4= ___ + × 3= ___ + × 2= ___ + × 1= ___

37 – 40 = Super!!!
32 – 36 = Excellent!!
27 – 31 = Good!
22 – 26 = Fair
 <22 = I need to work at this

Total _____

TEACHER'S SELF-EVALUATION: ESTABLISHING A SENSE OF PURPOSE

	ALMOST ALWAYS	USUALLY	SOME-TIMES	SELDOM or NEVER
1. Do I express confidence in my students' ability to succeed?				
2. Do I provide challenges for each student?				
3. Do I take time to discuss students' dreams and hopes with them?				
4. Do I provide opportunities for students to identify and focus on goals?				
5. Am I sensitive to students' lack of purpose and direction?				
6. Do I include work with values, and support positive values?				
7. Do I strive to take a less directive role as students demonstrate growth in taking initiative?				
8. Do I avoid placing students in competitive situations, which may frustrate work towards their goals?				
9. Do I encourage students to try new tasks and skills?				
10. Do I provide additional support when a student takes a bigger risk than usual?				

Subtotals ___ ___ ___ ___

× 4= ___ + × 3= ___ + × 2= ___ + × 1= ___

37 – 40 = Super!!!
32 – 36 = Excellent!!
27 – 31 = Good!
22 – 26 = Fair
 <22 = I need to work at this

Total _____

TEACHER'S SELF-EVALUATION: ESTABLISHING A SENSE OF COMPETENCE

	ALMOST ALWAYS	USUALLY	SOME-TIMES	SELDOM or NEVER
1. Do I give students opportunities to make choices or decisions?				
2. Do I help students assess the merits of different options relative to their goals?				
3. Do I encourage students by monitoring their progress with them?				
4. Do I plan experiences to expand students' knowledge of and use of various resources?				
5. Do I provide objective feedback rather than personal judgments?				
6. Do I help students assess their own progress and growth?				
7. Do I find ways to recognise students' accomplishments?				
8. Do I provide encouragement and recognition for students' progress as they work toward their goals?				
9. Do I make it clear in my classes that errors are a necessary part of the process of developing competence in language learning?				
10. Do I include activities for different learning styles, to give all my students opportunities to work in their own best ways?				

Subtotals   ___   ___   ___   ___

× 4= ___ + × 3= ___ + × 2= ___ + × 1= ___

37 – 40 = Super!!!
32 – 36 = Excellent!!
27 – 31 = Good!
22 – 26 = Fair
    <22 = I need to work at this

Total _____

References and further reading

Andrés, V. 1999. Self-esteem or the metamorphosis of butterflies, in J. Arnold (ed.) *Affect in Language Learning*. Cambridge University Press.

Andrés, V. 2007. Self-esteem and language learning: breaking the ice, in F. Rubio (qv).

Arnold, J., H. Puchta and M. Rinvolucri, 2007. *Imagine That! Mental imagery in the ELT classroom*. Helbling Languages.

Borba, M. 1989. *Esteem Builders: a self-esteem curriculum for improving student achievement, behavior & school-home climate*. Jalmar Press.

Borba, M, 1993. *Staff Esteem Builders*. Jalmar Press.

Branden, N. 1994. *The Six Pillars of Self-Esteem,* Bantam Books.

Canfield, J. 2005. *The Success Principles*. Harper Collins.

Canfield, J. and H. C. Wells, 1994. *100 Ways to Enhance Self-Concept in the Classroom*. Prentice-Hall.

Canfield, J. and F. Siccone, 1994. *101 Ways to Develop Student Self-Esteem and Responsibility.* Allyn & Bacon.

Coopersmith, S. 1967. *The Antecedents of Self-Esteem*. Freeman & Co.

Covington, M. 1989. Self-esteem and failure in school, in A. M Meera, N. J. Semiser and J. Vasconcellos (eds.) *The Social Importance of Self-Esteem*. University of California Press.

Dörnyei, Z. 2005. *The Psychology of the Language Learner: individual differences in language acquisition.* Lawrence Erlbaum Associates.

Dörnyei, Z. and T. Murphey, 2003. *Group Dynamics in the Language Classroom.* Cambridge University Press.

Ehrman, M. and Z. Dörnyei, 1998. *Interpersonal Dynamics in Second Language Education: The Visible and Invisible Classroom.* Sage.

Ellis, K. 2000. Perceived teacher confirmation: The development and validation of an instrument of two studies of the relationship to cognitive and affective learning, in *Human Communication Research* 26/2: 264-291.

Kagan, S. 1994. *Cooperative Learning.* Kagan Cooperative Learning.

Krashen, S. 1985. *The Input Hypothesis: issues and implications.* Longman.

León, I. 2005. *La confirmación del profesor de inglés percibido por el alumno en el aula de secundaria.* Unpublished doctoral thesis, University of Seville.

Markus, H. and A. Ruvolo, 1989. Possible Selves: personalized representations of goals, in L. A. Pervin (ed.) *Goal Concepts in Personality and Social Psychology.* Lawrence Erlbaum Associates.

References and further reading

Moskowitz, G. 1999. Enhancing personal development: humanistic activities at work, in J. Arnold (ed.) *Affect in Language Learning*. Cambridge University Press.

Murphy, T. 2006. *Language Hungry*. Helbling Languages.

Piñol, J. 2007. *La influencia de la confirmación del profesor en el aprendizaje de inglés en la Educación Secundaria Obligatoria*, Unpublished MA thesis, University of Seville.

Puchta, H. 1999. Creating a learning culture to which students want to belong: the application of neuro-linguistic programming to language teaching, in J. Arnold (ed.). *Affect in Language Learning*. Cambridge University Press.

Reasoner, R. 1982 *Building Self-Esteem: a comprehensive program*. Consulting Psychologists Press.

Reasoner, R. 1992. What´s behind self-esteem: you can bring hope to failing students, in *School Administrator* 49, (4):23:30.

Rodríguez, J., T. Plax and P. Kearney, 1996. Clarifying the relationship between teacher nonverbal immediacy and student cognitive learning: affective learning as the central causal mediator, in *Communication Education* 45: 294-305.

Rogers, C. 1969. *Freedom to Learn*. Charles E. Merrill.

Rubio, F. (ed.) 2007. *Self-Esteem and Foreign Language Learning*. Cambridge Scholars Press.

Stevick, E. 1980. *Teaching Languages: a way and ways*. Newbury House.

Wright, A. and D. Hill. 2008. *Writing Stories*. Helbling Languages.

Teacher's quick-reference guide

This guide will help you select an activity suitable for your class based on the time you have available and the learning level(s) of your students.

To use it, look down the left-hand column till you come to a time that's suitable for you, and then across to see the name of the activity spread across the range of levels it's suited to. Then across again to find the activity number.

Or if you prefer to start with the level of your students, go downwards till you find an activity name, and on that same row you will find the time required and the activity number. However, keep in mind that it is often easy to adapt activities for use with other levels.

Similarly, please note that the time guide is only very basic; it does not take account of any extension. It merely allows you to see, when you're thinking of doing an activity for the first time, approximately how long the activity is likely to take.

Teacher's quick-reference guide

Lesson time (mins)	Elementary	Lower intermediate	Intermediate	Upper intermediate	Advanced	Activity no
Chapter 1 A Sense of Security						
5			A focused mind			1.5
5				Listen to me (repeated)		1.7
5–10			What's your name?			1.2
5–10			1, 2, 3, stare!			1.4
10		Routines				1.1
10–15				Listen to me (first time)		1.7
30			A focused mind, variation			1.5
30–40				Seeds of confidence		1.3
30–40			The rules of the game			1.11
40–50				Welcoming exams		1.8
40–50				My mistake		1.9
40–50				Words that open, words that close		1.10
50				How do you frighten yourself?		1.6
15 + 15			My coat of arms			1.12
Chapter 2 A Sense of Identity						
15–20			True and false			2.3
20			Student of the week			2.2
20				A two-minute interview		2.8
20–30				Magic combs		2.9
30				Who are you three?		2.11
30–40			Talking about me			2.4
30–50		Circle time				2.5
40–50			Be yourself			2.6
40–50			A commercial about yourself			2.7
5–10 + 20–30			We bingo			2.1
20–30 + variable				The talking stick		2.10
Chapter 3 A Sense of Belonging						
5		Back to back				3.2
5–10		Groups or pairs				3.3
5–10		Take the weight off your shoulders				3.7
5–10		Hot potato				3.10

Teacher's quick-reference guide

Lesson time (mins)	Elementary	Lower intermediate	Intermediate	Upper intermediate	Advanced	Activity no
Chapter 3 A Sense of Belonging						
5–15	Line-ups					3.5
10	Mirroring					3.1
15	Marching together					3.4
20		Blindfold walk				3.8
20		Body shop				3.12
20–25		We perform				3.15
30–40		The leaders dance				3.13
40–50		Role-playing conflicts				3.6
40–50			Signs of the zodiac			3.14
40–50		Today's menu				3.16
50		Statues				3.11
10 + 20–30	The confidence corridor					3.9
Chapter 4 A Sense of Purpose						
Variable		Inspiring quotations				4.4
15		Help yourself				4.2
15			Visualise your goals			4.10
20		Words of affirmation				4.3
20			We can choose			4.13
20		My mission / life purpose statement				4.14
20	The end					4.15
25–35		Turning dreams into smart goals				4.9
25–40		Backward buildup				4.1
30		Eyes on the goal				4.5
30		What makes your heart sing?				4.8
30–40		Seeing your language self				4.11
40–50				Great dreams		4.7
40–50		A world of values				4.12
40–50			We can choose, variation			4.13
25 + 20–30			Formula for success			4.6

Teacher's quick-reference guide

Lesson time (mins)	Elementary	Lower intermediate	Intermediate	Upper intermediate	Advanced	Activity no
Chapter 5 A Sense of Competence						
Variable		My success log ———————————————————→				5.5
Variable	It's your choice ——————————————————————→					5.12
10			A/B success sharing ————————————→			5.1
10–15		Ping pong of talents ——————————————→				5.13
15			A happy day! ——————————————————→			5.10
20			The attitude of gratitude ——————————→			5.8
20–25		A gift for you ——————————————————→				5.9
30–45		My strengths ——————————————————→				5.14
40–50		.	Words have power! ——————————————→			5.2
40–50		Appreciation works! ————————————————→				5.6
40–50		A letter of acknowledgement ———————————→				5.7
50				Turning points: connecting the dots ———→		5.3
5–10 + 1–2 mins per student		The magic minute ——————————————————→				5.11
40–50 + variable		What I know ————————————————————→				5.4

Notes

Notes

The CD-ROM/Audio CD

The CD-ROM/Audio CD accompanying this book contains:

1. Worksheets and texts for use in class. You can print the material out or save it onto your computer.

Print / Save

2. Audio files with music tracks or imagery scripts to be used as part of several activities. All the audio files can be played directly from your computer or from a CD player.

3. Video files with short videos for some activities.

The following icons in the book will help you select files:

The CD-ROM can be projected on a screen from the computer or used with an interactive whiteboard.

The authors can be reached at:
http://www.veronica-andres.com
arnold@us.es